The Patriot's Handbook for Kids

An Activity Book

Super Citizens Who Made a Difference
Who, What, When, Where
You Know What?
Famous Words of Wisdom
Songs About America
(FREE Downloads)

Libby LIBERTY

Clovercroft Publishing

The Patriot's Handbook for Kids

©2016 by Liberty's Legacy, LLC

Published by Clovercroft Publishing, Franklin, Tennessee.

Cover Design by Suzanne Lawing

Interior Design by Adept Content Solutions

Edited by Jamie Chavez

Illustrated by Vickie Lee

Printed in the United States of America

978-1-942557-52-4

Introduction

My name is Libby and I live on Liberty Island in the New York harbor. I'm here to help you learn more about this great country. Inside this handbook, you can solve puzzles, enjoy word games, sing songs, and read stories about young people who became Super Citizens—some lived many years ago and some are kids just like you right now! There are also original songs you can download and sing as you enjoy these activities.

Over the years, I've seen millions of visitors who all share the dream of freedom and opportunity. That's the idea on which this country was founded. America is a melting pot of people from all over the world who came here because they wanted to have freedom.

As you learn about the history and the importance of this great nation, it's good to remember you will be the next generation of Americans to live by the ideals of the Founding Fathers and the other American heroes that you'll learn about on the following pages.

Remember: YOU are the next American Patriots!

Libby Liberty

To learn more about Libby Liberty and for FREE song downloads, visit http://libbyliberty.com

*"My fellow Americans: ask not what your country can do for you—
ask what you can do for your country."*

—John F. Kennedy

Super Citizens

Eliza Lucas Pinckney

born 1722

My favorite
subject is
botany...

Eliza Lucas's English parents owned 3 sugar farms on the island of Antigua in the British West Indies, but they sent Eliza and her 2 younger brothers, Thomas and George, to London for school. This was common for boys and not common for girls—but Eliza was smart, and her parents thought she should be educated. She studied French and music and grammar and botany (study of plants), which was her favorite subject. She wrote letters from England thanking her father for her education.

When Eliza was almost 16, the family moved to South Carolina, where her father had inherited 3 working plantations (farms) from his own father. The land was in the area around Charles Town (now Charleston), but still hours away from other people. The family would have to grow or make or scavenge anything they needed to survive. In addition, they would grow a "cash crop"—something to sell so they would have money to buy the things they couldn't make or grow themselves.

Eliza's father had to return to Antigua, and shortly after that, her mother died. Eliza was 16 years old—and she had to take over the plantation and 20 slaves, plus the 2 other plantations. Her younger brothers were still in London, but Eliza now had to care for her little sister too. She needed a cash crop, and began to experiment with growing indigo, a flowering plant used to make a dark blue dye for clothing.

And she succeeded. Indigo became the second largest crop in South Carolina (after rice). At age 22 Eliza Lucas married Charles Pinckney, a neighbor, and managed his plantations as well. Eliza Lucas Pinckney is noted as the first important agriculturalist (farmer) in the United States, and for the diary she kept, which tells a lot about life in the mid-1700s. She supported the American Revolution as a grown-up, and when she died, President George Washington was a pallbearer at her funeral in 1793.

Who, What, When, Where

★★★

How did Colonial Americans survive? The first settlers who came from England (and elsewhere) had to grow or make or scavenge everything they needed to live! Or they needed to buy things that came over from England.

Name 3 things Eliza's family might have made from fabrics.

_____

Name 3 things Eliza's family would make from wood.

_____

Name 3 things Eliza's family brought from England.

_____

Name 3 things Eliza's family produced themselves on the farm.

_____

Answers: Some things made with fabrics: clothing, towels, sheets, blankets, sails, curtains, furniture, rugs.
Some things made from wood: house, barn, boat, wagon, furniture, toys.
Some things brought from England: farm animals, tools, silverware, china, spices, tea, clothing, furniture.
Some things produced on the farm: soap, butter, food (by gardening), meat (by slaughtering livestock), eggs (from hens), thread for spinning, wagons, plows, flour (by grinding the meal).

Doodle Space

Who, What, When, Where

If you had a garden, what would you like to grow? Draw a picture of your garden here!

You Know What?

Eliza Pinckney told her father her favorite school subject was BOTANY. Today colleges often call this plant science or plant biology. No matter what you call it, this field is the study of plant life. If you go to a botanical garden, you can probably meet a botanist—and see hundreds of plant samples.

Who, What, When, Where

What's your favorite subject in school? Why?

_____

Word Search

★★

Here's a word search puzzle. If you lived on a southern colonial farm or plantation, you might grow these crops. Circle any words you find:

alfalfa	flax	lavender	rice
beans	ginger	oats	sugar
corn	hemp	peas	tobacco
cotton	indigo	potato	wheat

Look for 4 bonus words too!

```
M L V D R O H P P Y
T B E A N S A O E A
O B H E M P R T A L
B A S U M E S A S F
A R E B G T U T K A
C N I N D I G O C L
C P I C O W A N O F
O G B O E N R J T A
D F A R M G E L T Y
P L A N T A T I O N
R A N W H E A T N E
S X L A V E N D E R
```

Eliza Lucas Pinckney

Bonus words: plantation, cow, barn, farm

Indigo Plant
Color My World

Super Citizens

Nathan Hale

born 1755

ONLY REGRET THAT

Behind
enemy
lines...

Nathan Hale was born in 1755 in what is now Connecticut. When he was just 14 years old, he went with his brother, who was 16, to Yale College in New Haven, some 50 miles away—a long journey for two boys! It was unusual, too—most people couldn't afford to go to college in those days.

The Hale brothers enjoyed their time at the school. They made lots of friends. Years later, the people who knew Nathan—classmates, friends, relatives, teachers, and soldiers—remembered him and spoke well of him. Nathan Hale graduated from Yale in 1773 and became a teacher—at age 18. He was well-liked by his students too.

Two years later the Revolutionary War began, and Hale joined the militia in the summer of 1775. This was a big decision, as he would then be considered a traitor by the British—and he would be giving up a very good teaching job.

But Nathan Hale joined the Americans and served with Washington. In 1776, General Washington needed a spy behind enemy lines, and Hale was the only man who volunteered. It was important to the Americans to regain control of New York City, so Hale was ferried across the Long Island Sound. He knew it was a dangerous undertaking.

Ten days later, Nathan Hale was captured, and executed by hanging the very next day. It is said that in the shadow of the gallows he behaved with great calmness, and that he gave a speech in which he said, "I only regret that I have but one life to lose for my country"—although we don't know exactly what was said, because no records were kept. Nor was there ever a portrait of Nathan Hall, so we don't know what he looked like, either.

But at age 21, Nathan Hale became an American hero.

You Know What?

Yale College was originally founded to train ministers, in 1701, although by the time Nathan Hale got there, the curriculum also included the humanities (languages, literature, history, mathematics, and philosophy) and some natural science. It was renamed Yale University in 1887. Yale did not admit women until 1969.

Doodle Space

"I only regret I have but one life to lose for my country."

ONLY REGRET THAT

Color My World

Word Search

★★★

Here's a word search puzzle. Find words from the Super Citizen story
going across, down, or diagonally. Circle the words you find:

Yale	teacher	hanging	enlist
college	hero	Washington	enemy lines
spy	Connecticut	traitor	brother
New York	only one	honorable	army
Revolutionary	life	volunteer	

```
U G E N L I S T D A R M Y
W A S H I N G T O N O R A
V C O T F B N S H E A H L
D H Q J E K M P L N S A E
R O H F N E W Y O R K N Y
M N U L T R A I T O R G C
C O N N E C T I C U T I O
G R A I T U X S G W F N L
W A O N L Y O N E D R G L
K B S O T E A C H E R O E
U L V O L U N T E E R D G
L E N E M Y L I N E S T E
R D L J B R O T H E R N B
```

 **You Can Be a Super Citizen Too!**

★★★

How many ways can you think of to be a super citizen?

_____

_____

Famous Words of Wisdom

"I wish to be useful, and every kind of service necessary to the public good becomes honorable by being necessary."

—*Nathan Hale, to Captain William Hull prior to his spying mission*

Who, What, When, Where

★★

Statues of American heroes come in many varieties. Sometimes they are on a horse, sometimes they are standing. Sometimes they hold a torch or a book—or the hand of a child. If there were a statue of you, what would it look like? Draw it here!

Super Citizens

Joseph Plumb Martin

born 1760

Private Yankee Doodle: Eyewitness Account of the American Revolution

by Joseph Plumb Martin

Private Yankee Doodle

Joseph Plumb Martin was born in western Massachusetts in 1760, to a preacher, Ebenezer Martin, and his wife, Susannah Plumb. Joseph's parents sent him to live far away with his maternal grandparents when he was just 7 years old. They were having trouble making ends meet.

Joseph's grandparents were well-to-do, and at their house young Joseph received a good education, which included reading and writing. When the Americans went to war against the British, Joseph, now a teenager, was eager and ready to join the war. Many of his friends had gone to war, and he wanted to do the same. He was just 15.

Joseph's grandparents opposed his plan, but when he threatened to run away to join the navy, they gave their permission, and in June 1776 he signed up for 6 months with the local militia. He was assigned to New York City, and would have been there when Nathan Hale was captured and executed.

At the end of his 6 months, Joseph went home to his grandparents, but the excitement of battle proved too strong, and he enlisted again in 1777—this time in General Washington's Continental Army—and served until the end of the war in 1783. Joseph was present at many important Revolutionary War events, such as the battles of Brooklyn, Monmouth, and White Plains. He was encamped at Valley Forge with Washington, and was present at the siege of Yorktown and witnessed the British surrender there. He came home, later settled in Maine, married, and raised a family.

And there it might have ended. But Joseph Plumb Martin had been educated, and he kept a journal during the war—and in 1830 when he was an old man, he wrote and published a lengthy account of his time as an American soldier in the war for independence from Great Britain.

With a title like *A Narrative of Some of the Adventures, Dangers, and Sufferings of a Revolutionary Soldier, Interspersed with Anecdotes of Incidents That Occurred within His Own Observation*, it was not a best seller! But the book was rediscovered in the 1950s. Now historians have studied and verified the book, and it is considered an important resource for scholars who want to understand the American Revolution and what it was like. The book was republished in 1962 as *Private Yankee Doodle*.

You Know What?

The Statue of Liberty stats!

Full name: Liberty Enlightening the World
Address: Liberty Island (formerly Bedloe's Island), New York Harbor
Made of: copper
Represents: Libertas, the Roman goddess
Right hand holds: a torch, representing progress (enlightenment)
Left hand holds: a tablet, used to evoke the law, with the date
July 4, 1776
On her head: a crown that represents 7 seas and 7 continents
At her feet: the broken chains of tyranny
Height: 151 feet, 1 inch (from base to torch)
Pedestal height: 305 feet, 1 inch (from pedestal base to tip of torch)
Dedicated: 28 October 1886
And finally: in 1984 the Statue of Liberty was designated a UNESCO World Heritage Site!

Famous Words of Wisdom

"I saw the plundering British bands
Invade the fair Virginian lands.
I saw great Washington advance
With Americans and troops of France;
I saw the haughty Britons yield
And stack their muskets on the field."

—Joseph Plumb Martin, from "The Campaign of 1781" in Narrative ... of a Revolutionary Soldier, published in 1830

Word Search

★★★

Here's a word search puzzle. Find words from the Super Citizen story going across, down, or diagonally. Circle any words you find:

teenager	reader	enlisted	Washington
war	writer	Continental	journal
Valley Forge	education	Army	book
Yorktown	historian	soldier	British
navy	witness	general	

```
A E D U C A T I O N V S W B E
F H K P W R I T E R A N A V Y
C O N T I N E N T A L A R M Y
S B R I T I S H B C L D L Q O
J O U R N A L J O R E A D E R
M G E N E R A L O G Y I N U K
E N L I S T E D K R F J P L T
O X W A S H I N G T O N D S O
T P A R N H I S T O R I A N W
O M K H G T E E N A G E R F N
W S O L D I E R W D E C B A V
```

 # You Can Be a Super Citizen Too!

★★★

You could be a hero to someone who needs a friend. Is there a new student at school who seems shy? Is there a student who doesn't seem to have any friends? Why not be that friend?

You Know What?

You've sung the song called "Yankee Doodle," haven't you?

> Yankee Doodle went to town
> Riding on a pony;
> He stuck a feather in his hat,
> And called it macaroni.

We Americans consider it a song of pride and patriotism, but during Colonial times, the British used it to make fun of American soldiers. How? In those times, the word doodle meant "fool" or "simpleton." But those simple American farmers who became soldiers had the last laugh when the British were forced to surrender.

And there's another interesting word in this song—macaroni. Today you know macaroni as something you eat with cheese! But in the 1700s, rich men wore fancy wigs of curled hair. These were called Macaroni wigs. Who knew?

You Can Be a Super Citizen Too!

Do you know anyone who is a super citizen? List their names here.

_____

_____

_____

_____

Who, What, When, Where

★★★

What do you think of when you hear the song "Yankee Doodle"?
Draw a picture of a Yankee Doodle here.

You Know What?

"Yankee Doodle" is the state anthem of Connecticut.

Songs about America

The Yankee Doodle Boy

[https://www.youtube.com/watch?v=MN0FfjgRfW8]

This song was written by George M. Cohan, for his Broadway musical *Little Johnny Jones*, which opened in November 1904. It's often called "Yankee Doodle Dandy."

I'm a Yankee Doodle Dandy,
A Yankee Doodle, do or die;
A real live nephew of my Uncle Sam,
Born on the Fourth of July.
I've got a Yankee Doodle sweetheart,
She's my Yankee Doodle joy.
Yankee Doodle came to London, just to ride the ponies;
I am the Yankee Doodle Boy.

I'm the kid that's all the candy,
I'm a Yankee Doodle Dandy,
I'm glad I am,
So's Uncle Sam.
I'm a real live Yankee Doodle,
Made my name and fame and *boodle*,
Just like Mister Doodle did, by riding on a pony.
I love to listen to the Dixie strain,
I long to see the girl I left behind me;
That ain't a josh,
She's a Yankee, by gosh.
Oh, say can you see,
Anything about a Yankee that's a phony?

Super Citizens

Sybil Ludington

born 1761

The British are coming!

Wait—wasn't that Paul Revere who rode through the countryside to warn the colonial rebels that the British soldiers were coming? Yes, but Revere was a grown-up (age 40). Sybil Ludington rode more than twice the distance Paul Revere did, and she was only 16 years old!

The oldest of 12 children, Sybil grew up on a farm in New York (she was born in 1761). Her father, Henry Ludington, was an active citizen in their small town in addition to being a farmer and mill owner. When war came, he joined the militia for the American cause and soon became a colonel. (He was also a wanted man, because he was well-known to the British.) In April of 1777, a large British army moved nearby to Danbury, Connecticut. They left the property of British loyalists, but the army began burning everything that belonged to American rebels. A messenger was sent from Danbury to Colonel Ludington with news of the attack, reaching the home at nine o'clock that night—very late for a farming family.

It was planting season, and the men of the American regiment were all miles apart at their own farms. The Danbury messenger was too exhausted to continue, and, of course, he did not know the neighborhood. He would never find all the American soldiers. But Sybil—who had just turned 16—was very familiar with the area. She would have to avoid British loyalists and stray soldiers, and she would have to find remote farms—all in the middle of the night. It would be a very dangerous job. She left on her horse, Star, immediately, riding 40 miles through rain and the dark woods, alerting the soldiers. By daybreak, almost the whole regiment was gathered and able to fight the British troops as they moved through the area.

And that was it. After her ride, Sybil went back to helping out on the family farm. It's said that after the war, General Washington came to her house to thank her for her service. Some years later, she married, had children, and received a Revolutionary War pension. That's what we know. The only record of her heroism was written by her great-grandson many years later.

The British are coming!

Word Search

★★

Here's a word search puzzle. Find words from the Super Citizen story going across, down, or diagonally. Circle any words you find:

Revolutionary	soldier	creek	Star
War	horse	Danbury	Ludington
militia	stick	loyalist	*midnight ride
countryside	miles	rebels	(separate below)
British	gristmill	colonel	girl

*Words are separate in puzzle.

```
M O V R N P D A N B U R Y
A C G R I S T M I L L R D
C O L O N E L G S H A C E
L U D I N G T O N N J R U
J N K L S B E H O R S E F
W T M I L I T I A I A E B
B R I T S S T A R D E K R
E Y L R O U U W R E B H I
G S E B L O Y A L I S T T
I I S O D S T I C K E N I
R D V M I D N I G H T L S
L E O R E B E L S U P K H
R N W A R A N V T R Y S J
```

Famous Words of Wisdom

"Let me! I can ride as well as any man!"

—*Sybil Ludington*

Who, What, When, Where

★★

If you had to deliver a message all over your neighborhood, how would you do it? Would you ride your bike? Get your dad to drive you? Or maybe you live on a farm and you do have a horse you could ride, just like Sybil Ludington! Draw a picture of you delivering messages on the ride of your choice!

Who, What, When, Where

★★★

Can you match the US presidents with their nicknames?

1.	Lyndon Johnson	Old Rough and Ready
2.	John F. Kennedy	The Schoolmaster
3.	Abraham Lincoln	LBJ
4.	James Madison	The Great Emancipator
5.	Franklin Pierce	Father of the Constitution
6.	Ronald Reagan	Big Chief
7.	Franklin Roosevelt	Jack
8.	Theodore Roosevelt	Hero of San Juan Hill
9.	William Howard Taft	The American Talleyrand
10.	Zachary Taylor	Handsome Frank
11.	Martin Van Buren	Father of his Country
12.	George Washington	The Gipper
13.	Woodrow Wilson	FDR

Answers:
1. LBJ
2. Jack
3. The Great Emancipator
4. Father of the Constitution
5. Handsome Frank
6. The Gipper
7. FDR
8. Hero of San Juan Hill
9. Big Chief
10. Old Rough and Ready
11. The American Talleyrand
12. Father of his Country
13. The Schoolmaster

Super Citizens

Andrew Jackson

born 1767

From Colonial times to Western expansion

Andrew Jackson learned service to his country early in his life. He was born in the colonial era—1767—to poor parents who'd recently emigrated (moved) with 2 young sons from the Ulster province in Ireland. They ended up in the North/South Carolina area, where there were many Irish, and where their third son was born.

During the American Revolutionary War, Irish immigrants supported the American rebels; the oldest Jackson brother died in a battle defending South Carolina from the British. Andrew Jackson and his brother were couriers for the local militia (army), and when Andrew was just 13, the brothers were captured by the British.

They nearly starved to death while in prison. They also contracted smallpox during this time. When Andrew refused to clean the boots of a British soldier, the man took out his sword and slashed across his face, leaving him with a scar that ran along his right eye and cheek. Andrew Jackson had that scar for the rest of his life.

After the Revolutionary War, in the time historians call the "Western expansion" of the new country, Andrew Jackson went on to have a career as a lawyer and then became a military hero. His service for the United States in the War of 1812 showed his bravery and leadership skills, and earned him the nickname "Old Hickory." Later he became a politician, first in the Tennessee legislature and later as the 7th president of the United States. Andrew Jackson had a big personality, which gained him many friends … and many enemies. But he was always a fierce friend and defender of the United States, even when he was just a boy.

Famous Words of Wisdom

"Our Federal Union! It must be preserved!"

—*Andrew Jackson, in a toast at a celebration of Thomas Jefferson's birthday, 13 April 1830*

Old Hickory

Color My World

Word Search

★★

Here's a word search puzzle. Find words from the Super Citizen story going across, down, or diagonally. Circle any words you find:

president	lawyer	Ireland	bravery
revolutionary	hero	smallpox	life
war	fierce	boots	union
brother	rebels	scar	
Tennessee	prisoner	sword	
Old Hickory	capture	courier	

```
R E B E L S Z U N I O N A
T E N N E S S E E Y B H R
C P V P R E S I D E N T F
M F L O U S M A L L P O X
D I R E L A N D S S R L B
K E M T A U X O C W B D R
H R F P W D T R A O O H O
L C H G Y E L I R R O I T
I E D V E Q U L O D T C H
F C O U R I E R M N S K E
E U R C A P T U R E A O R
M A X P R I S O N E R R T
W T O S H B R A V E R Y Y
```

Who, What, When, Where

★★

There is a portrait of Andrew Jackson on the 20-dollar bill. Have you seen it? What if you were featured on American money? What would it look like? Draw yourself—or anybody you'd like to see—on a bill.

You Know What?

Here are some fun facts about Andrew Jackson!

• When he was 9 years old, he read the Declaration of Independence out loud to neighbors who had never learned to read.

• He killed a man in a duel—even though he was shot first. The bullet from that duel stayed in Jackson's chest for the rest of his life.

• He adopted 2 Native American boys in 1813. One boy died as an infant, the other died as a teenager.

• He won the popular vote for president 3 times—twice when he was elected and also in his first presidential run in 1824. This did not result in a majority of electoral votes, and he lost that election to John Quincy Adams.

• He was the first Irish-American president.

• He was the first president who did not come from a wealthy family.

• He was the first president who was a target for assassination.

• He loved to gamble—on dice, on cards, and on horse racing.

• The name of his home in Tennessee is the Hermitage.

Super Citizens

Frederick Douglass

born 1818

From slavery to civil rights activist

Frederick Douglass was born into slavery on a plantation (farm) in Maryland in 1818. By the age of 7 he had been taken away from both his mother and his grandmother—the only family he knew. At that time he was moved to another farm, where he worked until he was sent to his owner's brother in Baltimore.

This man's wife began to teach Frederick how to read when he was 12. The boy couldn't get enough of reading, because it opened up a whole new world. Even when Frederick's owner told his wife to stop the teaching, Frederick continued to secretly teach himself. Newspapers, the owner's children's books, things his master wrote … Frederick used all of these things to learn to read.

Soon Frederick was reading the Bible, and he began to teach other slaves on his farm and neighboring farms to read too. But some owners didn't want their slaves to read. Frederick would have to be stopped. They wanted to teach him a lesson …

So when he was just 15 years old, Frederick was sent to work for a hard man who had a reputation for breaking the spirits of young slaves. This man viciously beat the slaves until they were physically and psychologically broken; this made them do whatever he wanted them to.

This man whipped Frederick regularly, week after week, and he was successful with Frederick. Later Frederick would write he was "broken in body, soul, and spirit." But then there came the day that Frederick fought back. He was 16 years old, and "at this moment—from whence came the spirit, I don't know—I resolved to fight."

The fight lasted for 2 hours. The bad man's cousin fought with him, but the young, strong Frederick Douglass fought back—and won. Hitting a white man normally would bring severe punishment, but this man had a reputation to uphold. He did not want anyone to know he couldn't control a 16-year-old boy. So Frederick wasn't punished, then or ever.

Frederick Douglass would spend the rest of his life speaking out against slavery and for social reform; he became known all over the world. He was an excellent public speaker and writer. In 1872 he became the first African American nominated for vice president as the running mate for Victoria Woodhull, running on the Equal Rights Party ticket.

Before all this, though, Douglass was a slave for 5 more years; he escaped from the bad farmer in 1838 by hopping onto a train headed north. But—as he wrote in his book *My Bondage and My Freedom* (published in 1855)—"the day had passed forever when I could be a slave."

Word Search

★★

Here's a word search puzzle. Find words from the Super Citizen story going across, down, or diagonally. Circle any words you find:

slavery	reputation	freedom	boy
reading	speaker	broken	equal
Bible	writer	spirit	
Maryland	escape	train	
punishment	bondage	emancipation	

```
A W C P E Q U A L S A N
G R E A D I N G H B O Y
J I S P E A K E R I K R
S T R E P U T A T I O N
U E S C A P E A W Y B M
B R O K E N P N L H D A
O Z O G B I B L E S F R
N L H X C S L A V E R Y
D P U N I S H M E N T L
A O A F R E E D O M R A
G M T R A I N X D G K N
E N G T U S P I R I T D
```

Famous Words of Wisdom

"I would unite with anybody to do right; and with nobody to do wrong."

—*Frederick Douglass, in a lecture before the Rochester Ladies' Anti-Slavery Society, 1855*

Doodle Space

Who, What, When, Where

★★

Use the library or do some research online to answer these questions:

1. Was slavery legal in the 13 original colonies?

2. Was slavery legal in the United States of America?

3. Did some states abolish slavery? Which ones?

4. Which states were slave states?

5. Did all of those states secede from the Union?

6. When did the Civil War start?

7. When were the slaves freed?

Answers:

1. Yes. Slaves were brought to the colonies in the 1600s.

2. Yes. In spite of those self-evident truths, slavery was an issue that divided the Continental Congress; the Constitution could not pass with a ban on slavery. The compromises made to pass the Constitution ultimately led to the Civil War.

3. Yes, gradually. By 1804, all of the northern states at that time—Pennsylvania, New Hampshire, Massachusetts, Connecticut, Rhode Island, Vermont, New York, New Jersey—had abolished slavery or had plans in place to phase out slavery. Over the next 5 decades, though, every time a territory became a new state, there was a fight over whether it would be a "free state" or a "slave state."

4. Immediately prior to the Civil War, there were 34 states in the US, 15 of which were slave states: Texas, Arkansas, Louisiana, Mississippi, Alabama, Florida, Georgia, South Carolina, North Carolina, Virginia, Maryland, Delaware, Kentucky, Tennessee, and Missouri.

5. No, only 11 states seceded: Texas, Arkansas, Louisiana, Mississippi, Alabama, Florida, Georgia, South Carolina, North Carolina, Virginia, and Tennessee.

6. 12 April 1861.

7. President Abraham Lincoln issued a presidential proclamation and executive order—called the Emancipation Proclamation—on 1 January 1863 that changed the legal status of all enslaved people in the 10 southern states still in rebellion from slave to free. However, the proclamation was not a law passed by Congress. The 13th Amendment to the US Constitution—passed and ratified in 1865—abolished slavery in the United States for good.

Famous Words of Wisdom

"We hold these truths to be self-evident, that all men are created equal, that they are endowed by their Creator with certain unalienable Rights, that among these are Life, Liberty and the pursuit of Happiness."

—*The Declaration of Independence made by the Continental Congress, Philadelphia, Pennsylvania, 4 July 1776*

You Know What?

The word abolitionist comes from the root word abolish, which means "to get rid of completely." In America, abolitionists were people who opposed the practice of slavery—they wanted to completely get rid of slavery in this country. And they succeeded.

You Know What?

Here are some fun facts about Frederick Douglass:

• He traveled in Great Britain and Ireland for 2 years, raising funds for the abolitionist cause.

• He consulted with President Abraham Lincoln during the Civil War, and helped influence the Emancipation Proclmation.

• When President Lincoln died, Mrs. Lincoln sent his walking stick to Frederick Douglass.

• He founded and edited *The North Star*, an abolitionist newspaper.

• He was a strong supporter of the women's rights movement.

• He wrote 3 separate autobiographies.

• He was married twice, the second time to a white woman, which caused a scandal. To his critics, he said his first marriage had been to someone the color of his mother, and his second to someone the color of his father.

Famous Words of Wisdom

"I hold it that a little rebellion now and then is a good thing, and as necessary in the political world as storms in the physical."

— *Thomas Jefferson in a letter to James Madison, 30 January 1787*

Super Citizens

Clara Barton

born 1821

The most famous nurse who was never a real nurse...

As a little girl—she was born in Massachusetts in 1821—Clara Barton was very shy. She was happiest with her family, learning things at home from her older brothers and sisters.

When Clara was 10, her brother David fell off the roof of a barn and was seriously injured. Little Clara decided she would nurse David back to health. She learned how to measure and administer his medication, she helped him eat, and looked after him in every way. She even learned to "bleed" him with leeches (a standard treatment on those years). Even when the doctors had given up, Clara continued to care for her brother—and he made a full recovery.

This willingness to help others was strong in Clara, who became a schoolteacher at age 18. Soon she established a school for the children of her brother's millworkers, and later she founded the first free public school in New Jersey. When the Civil War began, Clara Barton began tending to wounded soldiers in Washington, DC, just as she had tended to her brother many years before.

In 1862, Clara's father was dying, and she returned home to help him. He encouraged her to continue her patriotic support of the troops. She was at many major battles, caring for the wounded in the field. After the war she spent 4 years searching for Union soldiers who'd died in the Civil War and been buried in unmarked graves.

Later, Clara Barton would learn about the International Red Cross. She was active in establishing the American society of the Red Cross. She also traveled to scenes of devastation where the Red Cross offered relief in the field—fires, hurricanes, tidal waves, explosions, famines. Although she was never trained as a nurse, Clara Barton is probably the most famous American nurse.

Famous Words of Wisdom

"I may be compelled to face danger, but never fear it, and while our soldiers can stand and fight, I can stand and feed and nurse them."

—*Clara Barton, during the Civil War*

Word Search

★★

Here's a word search puzzle. Find words from the Super Citizen story going across, down, or diagonally. Circle any words you find:

Red Cross   hurricane   soldiers   government
nurse   explosion   wounded   medication
schoolteacher   famine   battle   father
Civil War   fire   Washington   brother
sick   patriotic   DC

```
W A T H U R R I C A N E R
A M E D I C A T I O N E E
S O L D I E R S I P H S L
H W A G L P U S F C R U W
I O F I R E O B A U H M S
N U A R N L D E N R V O I
G N T C P A T R I O T I C
T D H X D L F A M I N E K
O E E I O R E D C R O S S
N D R O B A T T L E J Q S
D E H G O V E R N M E N T
C C I V I L W A R F N U A
S K B R O T H E R T W D F
```

Who, What, When, Where

★★

Clara Barton looked around and saw problems that needed to be solved. How about you? What problems do you want to solve when you grow up? Write about it here.

_____

_____

_____

_____

You Know What?

Here are some fun facts about nursing!

• The modern nursing profession is less than 150 years old in America.

• Before the modern era, nursing duties fell to nuns and monks or to the family of the sick person.

• Florence Nightingale was one of the first professional nurses in the modern era; she began practicing in the 1850s.

• Mary Todd Lincoln—President Lincoln's wife—was a volunteer nurse during the Civil War.

• Before the end of the 19th century, most nurses didn't have any formal training—they were trained on the job.

• A woman named Linda Richards was the first nurse to earn a professional nursing diploma in the US in 1873.

• You may know Walt Whitman as a famous American poet, but for 3 years during the Civil War he was a volunteer nurse!

Songs about America

You're a Grand Old Flag

[https://www.youtube.com/watch?v=rFV_tmTcU0Q]

George M. Cohan—an entertainer, playwright, composer, lyricist, actor, and singer-dancer—wrote this rousing number for his stage musical called *George Washington Jr.* The play opened in February of 1906, and the song's been a hit ever since.

> You're a grand old flag,
> You're a high-flying flag,
> And forever in peace may you wave.
> You're the emblem of the land I love,
> The home of the free and the brave.
> Ev'ry heart beats true
> 'Neath the Red, White and Blue,
> Where there's never a boast or brag.
> But should auld acquaintance be forgot,
> Keep your eye on the grand old flag.

Super Citizens

Harriet Hanson Robinson

born 1825

A Lowell mill girl becomes a suffragette...

When Harriet Hanson was 6 years old (she was born in 1825), her father died, leaving her mother to support the family by herself. There weren't a lot of jobs for women, so the family was very poor.

This was a problem for a lot of women in those days—but the Industrial Revolution in the United States provided a solution. As new technology was developed, the textile (cloth) industry became important. Power machines were developed to spin cotton and wool into thread and to weave the thread into cloth on electric looms. Before this, everything was done by hand. As businessmen tried to profit on the demand for fabric after the War of 1812 with the new machines, towns sprang up all over New England just for the textile industry.

One of the largest textile mills in the country was in Lowell, Massachusetts, a planned factory town just north of Boston. In these industry towns, young farm girls were recruited from all over to work in the mills. The factory owner built boarding houses for the girls to live in and hired older women to oversee and monitor the girls' behavior. There were cultural activities like libraries, concerts, Bible study groups, and clubs.

Harriet's mother was recruited to run a boarding house, and Harriet—at age 10—went to work in the mill to help support her family. (It was legal for children to have jobs in those days.) It seemed like a good life, but the girls were at the mercy of the mill owners— and the year Harriet was 11, the mill owner raised the rent without raising wages. This meant the girls made a lot less money!

So the mill girls went on strike—they walked out. Harriet, just a little girl, was one of the leaders, because she believed it was the right thing to do.

As it turned out, the strike failed, but Harriet went on to educate herself (as she continued to work in Lowell mills), to marry, and to become active in the women's suffrage (right to vote) movement. She was the first woman to testify before the Select Committee on Woman Suffrage in Congress in the winter of 1886–87.

Loom and Spindle

Color My World

Presidential Crossword Puzzle: Pairs!

These presidents have double letters in their names.

Across

1. There were 2 presidents by this name: grandfather and grandson.
2. A toy bear was named after this president.
3. The 13th President.
4. This president served on a PT boat in World War II.
5. This president was one of the Founding Fathers.

Down

1. A dam was named after this president.
2. This president was known as a man of few words.

Word Search

★★★

Here's a word search puzzle. Find words from the Super Citizen story going across, down, or diagonally. Circle any words you find:

Lowell	Boston	Industrial	New England
mill girls	technology	Revolution	strike
textiles	cotton	spinning	rent
women	wool	looms	suffrage

```
S M I L L G I R L S I U
W O O L Q U E P M B N A
O F L O W E L L C Y D R
M S P I N N I N G R U E
E J M L X D V O T E S V
N E W E N G L A N D T O
E B O S T O N D L S R L
C L F H N H L F O T I U
S B G H R E N T O R A T
A H C O T T O N M I L I
T E X T I L E S S K I O
T J S U F F R A G E K N
```

Famous Words of Wisdom

"Let us realize the arc of the moral universe is long but it bends toward justice."

— *Martin Luther King Jr., Address to the Southern Christian Leadership Conference, 16 August 1967*

You Know What?

What is a "suffragette"? It has to do with voting, and it comes from the word suffrage, which refers to the right or privilege of voting in political matters, such as the election of public officials. Although it might seem strange now, women did not have the right to vote in this country until the 19th Amendment to the Constitution passed in 1920. The women who worked hard to get the law changed were called suffragettes.

Who, What, When, Where

What kind of jobs (chores) do your parents ask you to do around the house? Do you think this is the same as working in a factory every day? How is your life different from Harriet's? How is your life the same as Harriet's? Write a paragraph about your work!

_____

_____

You Know What?

The Founding Fathers did a great job crafting the American Constitution, but as time went on, they noticed some additional clarification was needed. So the Constitution was amended (added to). The first 10 amendments are known as the Bill of Rights, but there are 27 amendments all together.

Vinnie Ream

born 1847

A young sculptor...

Like the president she would make famous in her art, Lavinia "Vinnie" Ream was born, in 1847, in a log cabin. Her family moved around a lot, because her father was a surveyor and a government map maker. She may have gotten her artistic talent from her father, but she had studied it in school too.

In 1861—Vinne was 14—the family moved to Washington, DC. When she was 15, she became one of the first women to be employed by the federal government: she helped support her family by working for the US Postal Service. Like many young women during that war, she spent time visiting hospitals to write letters for wounded soldiers or singing in hospital concerts and for churches.

Also during this time she visited the studio of famous sculptor Clark Mills, and got a job as an assistant in his workshop. Ream learned a lot from him, and developed many personal connections with important Washingtonians who visited the artist's studio. Soon she was able to take sculpting jobs herself—Congressman Thaddeus Stevens, journalist Horace Greeley, and Lieutenant Colonel George Armstrong Custer all sat for her.

So did President Lincoln. Vinnie Ream, with help from her important friends, convinced Lincoln to allow her to observe and sketch him as he worked for a half hour every morning … for 5 months. When the president was assassinated, Congress offered a commission (a job) for the creation of a statue in his honor—and Ream won the job based on the clay sculpture of Lincoln she'd been working on. She was 18 years old when she signed the contract, and 23 years old when the marble statue was unveiled.

This job was controversial, of course. Ream was the first woman and the youngest sculptor ever to earn a commission from the federal government. But it wasn't just that. Ream made a statue that looked like Lincoln—sad, tired, worn down by the war—in an age when many people thought statues of famous heroes should be idealized. He was dressed in his own clothing, rather than a Roman toga or a military uniform. Not everyone liked it. But Vinnie Ream gets the last laugh—the statue still stands in the US Capitol Building, 145 years later.

Famous Words of Wisdom

"I think that history is particularly correct in writing Lincoln down as the man of sorrow. The one great, lasting, all-dominating impression that I have always carried of Lincoln has been that of unfathomable sorrow, and it was this that I tried to put into my statue."

—*Vinnie Ream, quoted in "Personal Recollections of Lincoln...,"* Sunday Star, 9 February 1913, Washington, DC

Who, What, When, Where

★★★

If you were a sculptor, who would you sculpt? Draw a picture of your statue here.

Word Search

★★

Here's a word search puzzle. Find words from the Super Citizen story going across, down, or diagonally. Circle any words you find:

Lincoln	president	workshop	uniform
statue	log cabin	Congress	famous
sculptor	artistic	marble	hero
commission	assistant	honor	
Capitol	studio	bust	

```
W D H F W O R K S H O P M
C O N G R E S S T S R H A
A O Z H E R O N M C I S R
P S M R K G E T B U S T B
I T H M X D S S J L T U L
T Z U N I F O R M P A D E
O A S S I S T A N T T I F
L I E H D A S A V O U O A
G R H O N O R I T R E M M
P O C A L I N C O L N X O
S K L O G C A B I N F R U
A R T I S T I C O D D U S
```

Doodle Space

Presidential Crossword Puzzle: I C U!

These presidents all have their name's first letter in common.

Across

1. This is the only president to serve nonconsecutive terms in office.

Down

1. This president was governor of Arkansas before he became president.
2. This president was known as the peanut farmer.
3. Our 30th president.

Answers:

Across
1. Cleveland

Down
1. Clinton
2. Carter
3. Coolidge

Super Citizens

John Cook

born 1847

Johnny Cook earned a Medal of Honor at 15

Not much is known about John Cook's early life, but we do know he was born in Hamilton County, Ohio, in August 1847. This was a growing area with many villages, including Cincinnati, due to its location on the Ohio River. This was also along the way of the westward expansion. Hamilton County played an important role, during the first half of the 19th century, in the cultural development of Ohio.

By the time Johnny—because he was likely called by this nickname—was born, steamboats were manufactured in Cincinnati, and a medical college had been established there, in addition to hotels and restaurants and taverns. There were also social and cultural organizations that drew literary figures like Harriet Beecher Stowe, author of *Uncle Tom's Cabin*, who lived there during this period.

Because it was on the border with Kentucky—a slave state—emotions on the issue of the abolition of slavery ran very high in Hamilton County. So it's no surprise that Johnny Cook enlisted in the Union Army at age 14 as a bugler. Buglers and drummers conveyed signals and orders from the commanders to the troops; it was an important role. It's what a boy could do for his country.

Cook served in the 4th US Artillery and saw action at the Battle of Antietam Creek in 1862. The boy helped carry a wounded officer to the rear, and when he returned, the unit was under such heavy attack that most of the gunners were dead and the cannons were unused. Cook found ammunition and began to fire the cannons, continuing despite return fire from the Confederate troops.

The next year Cook saw action at the Battle of Gettysburg, carrying messages across difficult battle-torn terrain under heavy fire.

We can only imagine how it made Johnny Cook feel to serve at two of the bloodiest battles of the war—but we know he survived, and that at age 47 he was awarded the Medal of Honor, the American military's highest decoration, for his actions at the Battle of Antietam when he was just 15 years old.

Bugle Boy

You Know What?

Do you know how to pronounce Antietam? The word is thought to come from an Algonquian (Native American) Indian phrase that means "swift-flowing stream," and is pronounced "an-TEE-tum."

Famous Words of Wisdom

"As we lay there and the shells were flying over us, my thoughts went back to my home. I thought what a foolish boy I was to run away to get into such a mess I was in. I would have been glad to have seen my father coming after me."
—*Private Elisha Stockwell Jr., about the Battle of Shiloh, in his memoir* Sees the Civil War

You Know What?

The Battle of Antietam (sometimes called the Battle of Sharpsburg) was the first major battle in the Civil War to take place on Union soil. It happened near Antietam Creek in Maryland, and is still the bloodiest single-day battle in American history.

Word Search

★★★★★★★★★★★★★★★★★★★★★★★★★★★★★★★★★★★★★★★

Here's a word search puzzle. Find words from the Super Citizen story going across, down, or diagonally. Circle any words you find:

Antietam	Medal of Honor	bugler	creek
cannon	Gettysburg	artillery	home
Civil War	fifteen	war	
Hamilton County	boy	Union	
Ohio	service	Confederate	
Kentucky	battle	Maryland	

```
A S E R V I C E U T S Q F E
S O G F C I V I L W A R C D
T M E D A L O F H O N O R C
F E T C A N N O N U T R E B
I R T M O H I O G N I W E A
F O Y E L N S T U I E S K K
T O S K R G F I Z O T M G E
E N B A T T L E K N A A X N
E T U R A C O G D R M R U T
N S R A R T I L L E R Y E U
B U G L E R D D A S R L V C
N U R H O M E X G B W A R K
H A M I L T O N C O U N T Y
P O N L K J I H G Y B D A E
```

Doodle Space

Super Citizens

Orion Perseus Howe

born 1848

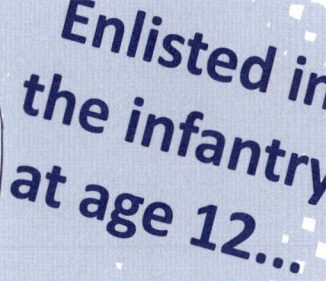

Enlisted in the infantry at age 12...

Orion Perseus Howe was born in rural Ohio in late December of 1848, but when his mother died 3 years later, his father, William, moved his two young sons to Waukegan, Illinois, north of Chicago.

William was a US Army veteran of the Mexican-American War of 1846–1847, and by the time of the Civil War was enlisted with the 55th Illinois Volunteer Infantry as the regimental bandleader. And in 1861, when Orion was 12, he and his younger brother left home to join their father in the army. Both boys were musicians; Orion was a drummer.

Two years later Orion participated in the Siege of Vicksburg in Mississippi. Vicksburg was the fortress city that held the last Confederate-controlled section of the Mississippi River. Control of the river was important, because it was a major north-south means of travel and commerce. If the Union could gain control of Vicksburg, troops could move right down the river to New Orleans. The Vicksburg campaign had been going on for months when the siege began in May of 1863.

The assault began on May 18. Casualties (injuries and deaths) were heavy. During the heat of battle on the 19th, Howe, along with other soldiers, was ordered to take a message to General Sherman: the regiment was out of ammunition. All of the messengers were killed and Howe was seriously injured, but he remained on the field of battle until he could report to General Sherman.

It took Orion Howe several months to recover, but he went back to the battlefield and was discharged in late 1864, when he was 15. He'd taken part in 14 battles. For his actions during the Siege of Vicksburg, he was awarded the Medal of Honor.

Civil War Drummer

Color My World

You Know What?

Doesn't this American hero have an interesting name? Let's break it down.

1. In Greek mythology, Orion was a giant huntsman; Zeus placed him among the stars as the constellation of Orion.

2. Perseus also comes from Greek mythology; he was the son of Zeus and as a grown man he killed Medusa. (There's a lot more—you should look it up!)

3. His last name, Howe, is English. In fact, William Howe, 5th Viscount Howe, was the commander-in-chief of British forces during the American Revolutionary War. (It's unlikely they're related though.)

Who, What, When, Where

Can you identify the constellation of Orion in the night sky? Have your parents show you, or look it up. Draw it here!

You Know What?

It was particularly dangerous to be a drummer boy, because the cadence they played communicated orders on the battlefield. If the enemy could kill the drummer, they shut down communications. Even when they survived, these young boys often had unhappy, unhealthy lives. Many of them died early.

Famous Words of Wisdom

"A drummer boy, 14 years of age, and severely wounded and exposed to a heavy fire from the enemy, he persistently remained upon the field of battle until he had reported to Gen. W. T. Sherman the necessity of supplying cartridges for the use of troops under command of Colonel Malmborg."

—*U.S. Medal of Honor Citation for Orion P. Howe*

Doodle Space

Word Search

Here's a word search puzzle. Find words from the Super Citizen story going across, down, or diagonally. Circle any words you find:

Orion	drummer boy	siege	ammunition
Perseus	battlefield	Illinois	boy
Howe	Medal of	infantry	constellation
Civil War	Honor	Mississippi	
musician	Vicksburg	River	

```
C Z A M U S I C I A N A Y
I O V I C K S B U R G M D
U R N S B X C T L S I M R
I I B S H O W E U R N U U
L O U I T R K E A V F N M
W N O S Y E S Q U E A I M
A H F S G R L B O Y N T E
R W S I E G E L O F T I R
K A N P A O L O A Y R O B
N B N P R I V E R T Y N O
H O Y I I L L I N O I S Y
A M E D A L O F H O N O R
Z B A T T L E F I E L D N
```

Super Citizens

Susie Baker King Taylor

born 1848

Early African-American Teacher

Susie Baker was born a slave on a plantation in Liberty County, Georgia, in 1848.

When she was 7, she traveled to Savannah about 20 miles away to live with her grandmother. Here she began to be educated, in spite of Georgia's strict and harsh laws against the education of African Americans. There were secret schools, and Susie attended two for a time. In those days, people who only had a little schooling would share what they knew, and this is how Susie learned to read and write and think.

After she had learned all she could from the school, Susie continued to learn from other people, both white and black—all of whom knowingly violated the law to teach her. Susie's education ended when the Civil War broke out.

Some of Susie's family fled with other African Americans to nearby St. Simons Island, because it was under the control of the Union Army. Here they claimed their freedom. Most African Americans, of course, were uneducated, so Susie's knowledge and intelligence stood out. Word spread, and within days, she was offered books and school supplies if she would organize a school. And that is how, at age 14, Susie Baker became the first black teacher to openly instruct African Americans in Georgia!

By day Susie taught children; by night she taught adults. This is how she met her first husband, Edward King, a black soldier in the Union Army. For the next 3 years, Susie traveled with her husband's regiment; she worked for the army as a nurse and a laundress, but she also taught black Union soldiers how to read and write. She was never paid for this work.

Susie was still a teenager when the war ended and she returned to Savannah with her husband, where she established another school for black children. Later she helped organize the Women's Releif Corps, a group that provided assistance to hospitals and soldiers. When she was an older woman, Susie Baker King Taylor published a memoir of her experiences during the Civil War.

Word Search

★★★

Here's a word search puzzle. Find words from the Super Citizen story going across, down, or diagonally. Circle any words you find:

plantation	county	write	freedom
liberty	secret	soldier	Civil War
Georgia	school	regiment	
education	teacher	nurse	
Savannah	read	army	

```
S C I V I L W A R D E
G O R E G I M E N T S
E E D U C A T I O N A
O D S C H O O L O U V
R E N S O L D I E R A
G S E C R E T B W S N
I L K R S A E E R E N
A G O N T R A R I L A
C O U N T Y C T T A H
E L A M O P H Y E R T
H L U F R E E D O M E
P R E A D G R F B Y R
```

You Know What?

〰〰〰〰〰〰〰〰〰〰〰〰〰〰〰〰〰〰〰〰〰〰〰〰〰〰〰〰〰〰〰

The United States Congress formally recognized the Pledge of Allegiance for the first time on June 22, 1942: I pledge allegiance to the flag of the United States of America, and to the Republic for which it stands, one Nation indivisible, with liberty and justice for all. Congress passed a law, which added the words "Under God" in 1954.

You Know What?

Liberty County, Georgia, was established in 1777 and named Liberty for the American ideal of freedom. We might wonder what the enslaved people thought about this.

Who, What, When, Where

We are lucky to live in a country that now provides education for all children. But it wasn't always that way. Susie Baker King Taylor had to break the law to get an education. Make a list of all the things you learned in school this year. Remember to say thank you to your teachers!

_____   _____

_____   _____

_____   _____

_____   _____

_____   _____

Famous Words of Wisdom

"I do not condemn all of the Caucasuan race because the Negro is badly treated by a few."
—*Susie Baker King Taylor,* Reminiscences of My Life in Camp with the 33rd U.S. Colored Troops, Late 1st South Carolina Volunteers, *1902*

Presidential Crossword Puzzle: Presidential Cities!

These American cities share their name with US presidents. Hints are the state where the city is located, and the first letter of the city name.

Across
1. Ohio: C
2. District of Columbia: W
3. Louisiana: M
4. Mississippi: J
5. Arkansas: V

Down
1. Nebraska: L
2. Wisconsin: M

Answers:

Across	Down
1. Cleveland	1. Lincoln
2. Washington	2. Madison
3. Monroe	
4. Jackson	
5. Van Buren	

Super Citizens

Nellie Bly

born 1864

The first investigative journalist!

Nellie Bly—a pen name—was born Elizabeth Cochrane in 1864, near Pittsburgh, Pennsylvania, to a very large family. This meant the children had to look after themselves a lot—especially after their father died. Watching her mother struggle to make ends meet made Elizabeth strong and independent, even as she helped her mother run a boardinghouse in Pittsburgh.

When the *Pittsburgh Dispatch* newspaper ran an article called "What Girls Are Good For" which called working women "monstrosities," Elizabeth fired off an angry letter to the editor. She used her first pen name—"Lonely Orphan Girl"—and she was just 16 years old.

But she made her point. The editor of the newspaper was impressed with her. He ran an advertisement seeking the identity of Lonely Orphan Girl. As soon as Elizabeth introduced herself, the editor asked her to write another article. It was a good one, too, and at the age of 18, Lonely Orphan Girl was offered a full-time job writing for the *Pittsburgh Dispatch*.

In those days—the 1880s—pen names were common for newspaper writers (men and women, though it was much more common for women). It was decided that Elizabeth needed a name that was "neat and catchy." The name Nellie Bly—made famous by one of Pittsburgh's most famous residents, the songwriter Stephen Foster—was chosen.

Nellie Bly's early stories for the *Dispatch* focused on the difficulties of being a working woman, but eventually—at age 21—Nellie left for New York City and a job at Joseph Pulitzer's newspaper, the *New York World*. It was here that she would make her name as an investigative reporter, going undercover to get stories no one else could get. The sensational stories got a lot of attention.

Later Nellie Bly would undertake to repeat the trip recounted in Jules Verne's novel *Around the World in Eighty Days*. She made the trip in 72 days, alone, and returned to New York the most famous woman on earth. She was 25 years old.

Investigative Journalist

Color My World

Famous Words of Wisdom

"Very well. Start the man and I'll start the same day for some other newspaper and beat him."

—*Nellie Bly, to her editor at the* New York World, *when she heard they were going to send a man around the world.*

You Know What?

Nellie Bly carried only 1 piece of luggage on her trip around the world, and it was very small—just 16 inches wide and 7 inches high! What was inside? 2 traveling caps, 3 veils, a pair of slippers, toilet articles, an ink stand, pens, pencils, paper, pins, needles, thread, a dressing gown, a tennis blazer, a small flask, a drinking cup, a few changes of underwear, handkerchiefs, and a jar of cold cream!

Famous Words of Wisdom

"Liberty and Union, now and forever, one and inseparable!"

—*Daniel Webster (of Massachusetts), in a Senate debate with Robert Y. Hayne of South Carolina*

Word Search

★★

Here's a word search puzzle. Find words from the Super Citizen story going across, down, or diagonally. Circle any words you find:

investigative	newspaper	byline	girl
journalist	dispatch	article	headlines
woman	world	writer	editor
pen name	undercover	reporter	job
Pittsburgh	newsroom	makes	
New York	working	trip	

```
I S A R T I C L E W H O B
G N E W S P A P E R L E Y
B E V O N W O R K I N G L
U W R E D I T O R T S L I
N S E G S F M A K E S A N
D R P I T T S B U R G H E
E O O R J D I S P A T C H
R O R L O S T G W O R L D
C M T I B W O M A N F H M
O P E N N A M E D T R I P
V O R J O U R N A L I S T
E S N U N E W Y O R K V P
R H E A D L I N E S L M E
```

Songs about America

When Johnny Comes Marching Home
[https://www.youtube.com/watch?v=4tIsXLyZcWI]

This song was popular during the Civil War, because almost everyone knew someone who was away from home, fighting in the war. The words were written by Patrick Gilmore, a bandleader who borrowed the music from an old tune that had been around for 200 years. It was published in 1863.

When Johnny comes marching home again
Hurrah! Hurrah!
We'll give him a hearty welcome then
Hurrah! Hurrah!
The men will cheer and the boys will shout
The ladies they will all turn out
And we'll all feel gay
When Johnny comes marching home.

The old church bell will peal with joy
Hurrah! Hurrah!
To welcome home our darling boy,
Hurrah! Hurrah!
The village lads and lassies say
With roses they will strew the way,
And we'll all feel gay
When Johnny comes marching home.

Super Citizens

Carlos Montezuma

born 1866

Bridging
two
cultures...

Carlos Montezuma's name was Wassaja (it means "signaling") when he was born in the mid 1860s in the Arizona Territory. His parents were Yavapai Indians—Native Americans. His father was a chief. It was a very unsettled time in Arizona history, and as a little boy, Wassaja was stolen from his family by Pima Indian warriors. He never saw any of his family again.

This was in 1871—the same year a traveling photographer was visiting Arizona. Carlos Gentile had emigrated from Italy to the United States in the 1850s; he was traveling through the Southwest taking photographs of the native people, recording their society and culture on film.

The Pima wanted to sell the little boy as a slave. To save him, Gentile purchased him for 30 dollars, and treated him as his son. He named the boy Carlos Montezuma, after himself and the famous Aztec emperor. For a few years, Carlos Montezuma lived in and around Chicago with his Italian "father," and there he had a chance to go to school. He was very smart, and loved to learn.

When Gentile lost all his belongings in a house fire, he had to go back on the road to earn a living. And he had to make a decision. Should he take his son with him and interrupt his schooling? Or should he find a stable home for him? Gentile asked the Indian Department of the American Baptist Home Mission for help, and Carlos Montezuma went to Urbana, Illinois, to live in the home of a Baptist minister.

Here Carlos graduated from high school and entered the University of Illinois in 1880, when he was around 14 years of age. At the university he studied lots of things, but he excelled at chemistry. In 4 years, Monte—as his friends called him—graduated and moved to Chicago, where he went to the Chicago Medical College at Northwestern University. He had been the first Native American student at the University of Illinois and at Northwestern. In 1889 he became the first Native American ever to earn a medical degree at an American university.

Carlos Montezuma went on to work as a doctor for the US Bureau of Indian Affairs and to be a lifelong activist for the rights of Native Americans.

Word Search

★★

Here's a word search puzzle. Find words from the Super Citizen story going across, down, or diagonally. Circle any words you find:

Arizona	doctor	photograph	culture
Yavapai	medical	Italy	*make fire
college	degree	territory	(separate below)
university	Montezuma	Indian	boy
Chicago	warrior	family	
Illinois	society	Native American	

*Words are separate in puzzle.

```
N T E R R I T O R Y P H A T
S A L C U L T U R E H N R C
H U T E H F D O C T O R G O
I N D I A N B S A Z T W I L
F I Y A V A P A I D O A G L
O V U S L E P R D E G R E E
N E B O Y F A T E M R R O G
D R I C L A D M O G A I L E
A S G I S M A K E H P O N I
F I R E D I N T F R H R U T
H T M T I L L I N O I S T A
L Y Z Y G Y B M E D I C A L
A S R D M O N T E Z U M A Y
C H I C A G O L U M T R G N
```

You Know What?

◆◆◆

The name Yavapai means "people of the sun"—but do you know how to pronounce it? "YAH-va-pie."

First Native American Doctor

Songs about America

This Land Is Your Land

[https://www.youtube.com/watch?v=WGKU8awk7Vg]

American folk singer Woody Guthrie wrote "This Land Is Your Land" in 1940 as a response to Irving Berlin's popular song "God Bless America"—because he was tired of hearing it!

This land is your land, this land is my land
From California to the New York Island
From the Redwood Forest to the Gulf Stream waters
This land was made for you and me.

As I was walking that ribbon of highway
I saw above me that endless skyway
I saw below me that golden valley
This land was made for you and me.

I roamed and I rambled and I followed my footsteps
To the sparkling sands of her diamond deserts
While all around me a voice was sounding
This land was made for you and me.

When the sun came shining, and I was strolling
And the wheat fields waving and the dust clouds rolling
A voice was chanting, as the fog was lifting,
This land was made for you and me.

Famous Words of Wisdom

"If the world be against us, let us die on the pathway that leads to the emancipation of our race; keeping in our hearts that our children will pass over our graves to victory."

—Dr. Carlos Montezuma, Native American activist

 # You Can Be a Super Citizen Too!

★★

A super citizen obeys the law. That means the laws of the United States of America, and the rules of your school and your parents. Do you obey your teachers and parents?

Doodle Space

Super Citizens

Audie Murphy

born 1925

Most decorated American solider in WWII...

In 1925, Audie Murphy was born into a poor sharecropper's family in northeast Texas. It was a rough life—he had 11 brothers and sisters; 6 were older than him. His father eventually deserted his wife and family.

To help support the family, Audie dropped out of school in fifth grade, when he was 10. He got a job picking cotton for a dollar a day. He also became very good with a rifle, hunting small game like squirrels and rabbits to keep food on the table. This would prove a useful skill when he became a soldier.

When he was just 16 years old, Audie's mother died, and his 3 youngest siblings were put into foster care. And then the attack on Pearl Harbor happened.

Like many young men at that time, Audie was ready to serve his country. But he was too small and too young to meet the requirements for the marines and the navy. So—again, like many young men at that moment in history—Audie lied about his age and was accepted by the US Army.

Audie shipped out to the European theater of war and was stationed in Italy and France. He immediately distinguished himself with his bravery and his sharpshooting. One of his most well-known actions happened in France, when his tank unit was attacked and outnumbered. When the crew was forced to abandon the tank, Audie returned to it and fired on the advancing Germans. For his actions that day, he was awarded the Medal of Honor.

In fact, Audie received every US military combat award for bravery available from the US Army for his World War II service. He was called "the most decorated soldier in America." He also received medals from France and Belgium.

You Know What?

The Medal of Honor is awarded by the President of the United States in the name of the US Congress, to military personnel who have performed personal acts of valor (bravery) "above and beyond the call of duty." It is the United States of America's highest military honor.

"They were killing my friends."
—*Audie Murphy, when asked why he had seized the tank machine gun, as quoted in* Stars and Stripes

You Know What?

On December 7, 1941, 353 Japanese fighter planes, bombers, and torpedo planes attacked the naval base at Pearl Harbor, Hawaii. It was a surprise attack, and it came as a shock to the American people. This action led directly to the US entering World War II. President Franklin D. Roosevelt said that December 7th was "a date that will live in infamy."

Word Search

Here's a word search puzzle. Find words from the Super Citizen story going across, down, or diagonally. Circle any words you find:

sharecropper	bravery	Marines	tank
decorated	Italy	Pearl Harbor	valor
medal of honor	France	requirements	hero
Texas	Army	soldier	crew
poor	Navy	war	military
farmer			

```
G M E D A L O F H O N O R
Z I H E R O N C R E W S L
A L D C F B A T Y G T H A
T I P O O R G D M N R A S
S T H R T A N K E W A R B
O A O A R V Y M H S G E L
L R A T D E E F R A N C E
D Y W E T R F A R M E R D
I S O D I Y H O V A L O R
E R L U M A R I N E S P N
R P Q R T E X A S F I P A
P E A R L H A R B O R E V
R B I T A L Y O G N S R Y
```

You Know What?

A sharecropper is someone who farms land and pays rent to the landowner in the form of a portion, or share, of the crops produced.

Most Decorated Soldier in WWII

You Know What?

The single most decorated soldier in American history is Colonel Robert L. Howard (1939–2009). Col. Howard was wounded 14 times over 54 months of combat in Vietnam, and was awarded the Medal of Honor, 8 Purple Hearts, 1 Distinguished Service Cross, 1 Silver Star, 4 Bronze Stars, and many others. (He was nominated for the Medal of Honor 3 separate times.) He served 50 years in the United States Army, and is buried in Arlington National Cemetery.

Who, What, When, Where

Why is the US Capitol building so important? Draw it here!

Super Citizens

Calvin Graham

born 1930

The boy who became a WWII veteran at 13...

Calvin Graham was born in Texas in 1930, the youngest of the 7 children in a farm family. When the kids' father died, their mother remarried to an abusive, unloving man. Calvin stayed out of the house as much as possible, selling newspapers and delivering telegrams after school and on weekends.

When the Japanese bombed Pearl Harbor in World War II, Calvin was 11 (he must have looked older)—and he was ready to go fight the war. He was underage, but that wasn't a problem for Calvin: he forged his mother's signature on a permission slip and told his mom he was going to visit relatives for a while!

A lot of American boys wanted to serve in World War II, and it wasn't uncommon for them to lie about their age. Often they came from large, poor families without enough food to go around. (Remember, the country had just come through the Great Depression.) Other boys had family problems and they just wanted to get away. In Calvin Graham's case, it was both.

Eventually Graham was sworn into the Navy. He was 12 years, 4 months and 12 days old on that day—15 August 1942—the youngest person to enlist in the US military since the Civil War. After basic training, he sailed as a gunner on the battleship *USS South Dakota* out of Philadelphia to the South Pacific.

There the *South Dakota* engaged in the bloody naval battle of Guadalcanal and was nearly destroyed by 42 direct hits. It was one of World War II's most ferocious battles at sea, and the ship would become one of the most decorated warships in navy history.

During the battle, Graham was knocked down three stories of superstructure and hit by shrapnel. He got to his feet and spent the long night giving aid to the wounded. For his efforts, Graham was later awarded the Bronze Star and a Purple Heart, when the already legendary *South Dakota* returned to New York for repairs.

But when Graham's mother saw him in a newsreel (movie), she reported him to the navy, and at age 13, he was discharged—the nation's youngest World War II veteran.

Who, What, When, Where

★★

How are the colors, stripes, and stars on the US flag meaningful?
Draw it here!

Word Search

★★★

Here's a word search puzzle. Find words from the Super Citizen story going across, down, or diagonally. Circle any words you find:

South Dakota	Purple Heart	Pearl Harbor	enlist
Guadalcanal	Bronze Star	lie	military
South Pacific	battleship	shrapnel	boy
navy	sea	permission	poor
veteran	Texas	newsreel	

```
S I B R O N Z E S T A R Y
S O U T H D A K O T A S O
B P U Z I P O O R U B H G
A E D T H U M L I E P R U
T A G N H R B A F T E A A
T R E E Z P N I M E R P D
L L N W O L A T I R M N A
E H L S L E V C L A I E L
S A I R N H Y D I N S L C
H R S E S E A N T F S G A
I B T E X A S T A Y I R N
P O F L S R O A R T O C A
G R I D R T B O Y I N A L
```

Battleship Gunner

Color My World

You Know What?

The Three Branches of the U.S. Government

The Constitution of the United States divides the federal government into three branches to ensure a central government in which no individual or group gains too much control:

- Legislative – Makes laws (Congress)
- Executive – Carries out laws (President, Vice President, Cabinet)
- Judicial – Evaluates laws (Supreme Court and Other Courts)

Legislative Branch

The legislative branch enacts legislation, confirms or rejects presidential appointments, and has the authority to declare war.

- Senate - There are two elected senators per state, totaling 100 senators.
- House of Representatives - There are 435 elected representatives.

Executive Branch

The executive branch carries out and enforces laws. It includes the president, vice president, the Cabinet, executive departments, independent agencies, and other boards, commissions, and committees.

Key roles of the executive branch include:

- President - The president leads the country. He/she is the head of state, leader of the federal government, and commander-in-chief of the United States Armed Forces. The president serves a four-year term and can only be elected two times.
- Vice President - The vice president supports the president. If the president is unable to serve, the vice president becomes president.
- The Cabinet - Cabinet members serve as advisors to the president. They include the vice president and the heads of executive departments.

Judicial Branch

The judicial branch interprets the meaning of laws, applies laws to individual cases, and decides if laws violate the Constitution.

The judicial branch is comprised of the Supreme Court and other federal courts.

- Supreme Court - The Supreme Court is the highest court in the United States.
- Other Federal Courts - The Constitution grants Congress the authority to establish other federal courts.

https://www.usa.gov/branches-of-government

Super Citizens

Sylvia Mendez

born 1936

Separate
is never
equal...

Sylvia Mendez's parents arrived in the United States in the 1920s—as a Puerto Rican, her mother was an American citizen and her father, a Mexican immigrant, was a naturalized US citizen—and though they had little when they arrived, they grew successful in business.

But at that time in American history, most southern and southwestern schools were segregated (kept separate). In the South, black children were segregated from white children. In the Southwest—New Mexico, Arizona, California, Nevada, Utah, and Colorado—Latino children were segregated from white children. (Latino refers to people from Latin America, such as Cubans, Puerto Ricans, Mexicans, and those from Central or South America.)

Sylvia was born in California in 1936, and soon her family moved to the town of Westminster. There were two schools in Westminster: one was a two-room shack in the Mexican neighborhood, while the other had a beautiful lawn and a very nice playground. The Mendezes wanted Sylvia and her two brothers to go to the nice school, but they were refused because of their skin color.

So in 1945, Mendez's parents and others filed a lawsuit to desegregate the schools in Westminster. Soon they were joined by others, including the National Association for the Advancement of Colored People (NAACP) and the Japanese American Citizens League. All of these people had children who were being segregated into substandard schools.

The Mendez lawsuit was won in 1946 and upheld on appeal in 1947. This case immediately desegregated schools in California— the first state in the union to do so—and it set the stage for the more famous *Brown v. Board of Education* lawsuit 7 years later. More importantly, it influenced the thinking of the then-governor of California, Earl Warren, who was chief justice of the Supreme Court when Brown brought an end to school segregation in the entire country.

At age 11, Sylvia Mendez at last had the right to go to the good school—and she became one of the first Latino children to attend an all-white school in California. It wasn't easy for her (many of the other children called her names and picked on her), but she went anyway—and she went all the way to graduate from college. In 2011, Sylvia Mendez was awarded the Presidential Medal of Freedom.

Famous Words of Wisdom

"I started crying and I [went] home and [told] my mother, 'They don't want us in that school,' and my mother said, 'We're going to fight for you, because you're just as good as they are and we're all equal under God! Of course you're going to go to that school.'"

—*Sylvia Mendez, on the occasion of receiving the Presidential Medal of Freedom*

You Know What?

Laura Ingalls Wilder really did live in a little house on the prairie! And when she was not quite 16 years old, she became a teacher in a one-room schoolhouse in South Dakota. She was in her 60s when she published her first book, *Little House in the Big Woods*.

Famous Words of Wisdom

"Let every nation know, whether it wishes us well or ill, that we shall pay any price, bear any burden, meet any hardship, support any friend, oppose any foe, in order to assure the survival and the success of liberty."

—*John F. Kennedy, Inaugural Address, 20 January 1961*

Presidential Medal of Freedom

Color My World

Word Search

★★

Here's a word search puzzle. Find words from the Super Citizen story going across, down, or diagonally. Circle any words you find:

segregate

California

Latino

Medal of Freedom

*American citizen
(separate below)

neighborhood

Westminster

school

lawsuit

Supreme Court

important

children

white

black

brown

years

immigrant

sue

*Words are separate in puzzle.

```
B Z N D X F L U B G P I N M
A M E R I C A N L O R M O S
W H I T E H Y E A R S D F U
E N G I D B M Q C L E A Y P
S C H O O L E A K E G H I R
T I B L I M P O R T A N T E
M R O C A L I F O R N I A M
I B R O W N F R O A H L Y E
N R H N S O C I T I Z E N C
S G O T L A T I N O R S T O
T Z O A I M M I G R A N T U
E O D E S E G R E G A T E R
R E F L U C H I L D R E N T
M D H O E Y R L A W S U I T
```

You Know What?

Have you heard your teacher say America is a melting pot? What does that mean? Think of a pot on the stove to which the cook adds many different kinds of cheese—some cheeses are orange, some are yellow, some are tan, some are white. But as they melt together on the stove, they become one big pot of cheese! So this phrase means that America as we know it is a nation of immigrants—people who come from all over the world to live in the United States and to become American citizens.

Doodle Space

 ## You Can Be a Super Citizen Too!

★★

A super citizen shows respect to humans and animals. Always!

Ryan White

born 1971

Presidential Commission on AIDS

A sick boy helps the country learn the truth about disease...

Ryan White was born in Kokomo, Indiana, in 1971, and when he was 3 days old he was diagnosed with hemophilia. This is a hereditary, incurable disease of the blood—because it is missing an important ingredient, the blood doesn't clot, so the hemophiliac is in constant danger of bleeding. To treat hemophilia, patients receive blood transfusions that contain the missing ingredient.

Ryan was healthy for most of his childhood, but when he was 13 years old, he got very sick with pneumonia and was diagnosed with the HIV/AIDS virus. How did Ryan get a deadly, little-known virus? In the hospital—from his routine blood transfusions.

At that time, the scientific community knew next to nothing about AIDS (and because of that, a diagnosis was considered a death sentence). Doctors didn't know how to test for AIDS, but they quickly learned that blood stored in hospitals everywhere was contaminated.

AIDS had quickly become an epidemic in the early 1980s. People all over the country were frightened, even though as time went on, many things were learned about AIDS. In particular, scientists learned that it is perfectly safe to be around people with AIDS, just as it is perfectly safe to be around people who have cancer.

As Ryan recovered from the pneumonia, he wanted to go back to school—but due to ignorance and fear, he was not allowed to return to school. The White family filed a lawsuit to overturn the school's decision, and several months later the school was ordered to readmit Ryan.

This created unbearable tension in the Kokomo community. The White family and their supporters received death threats. Finally, they moved to another town, where Ryan was able to go back to school in peace.

The publicity from the trial brought a lot of attention to Ryan. He appeared on national television and participated in many fund-raising activities to help find a cure for AIDS. In 1988, Ryan spoke before the President's Commission on the HIV Epidemic in Washington, DC.

Although he died in 1990 at age 18, Ryan White left a strong legacy of speaking out to effect change. He had helped change public perception of his disease. Later AIDS activist Larry Kramer said, "I think little Ryan White probably did more to change the face of this illness and to move people than anyone." And 4 months after his death, the US Congress enacted the Ryan White CARE Act, which funds programs to improve the availability of care for low-income, uninsured, or underinsured AIDS patients.

Famous Words of Wisdom

"The thing that we need in the world today is a group of men and women who will stand up for right and to be opposed to wrong, wherever it is. A group of people who have come to see that some things are wrong, whether they're never caught up with. And some things are right, whether nobody sees you doing them or not."

—Martin Luther King Jr., "Rediscovering Lost Values," a sermon, 28 February 1954

Doodle Space

Word Search

★★★

Here's a word search puzzle. Find words from the Super Citizen story going across, down, or diagonally. Circle any words you find:

KoKomo	AIDS	trial
epidemic	illness	Congress
disease	school	cure
hemophilia	scientist	clot
transfusion	publicity	bleeding
blood	legacy	decision

```
N C O N G R E S S E L N
P E S C H O O L A P O C
U H E M O P H I L I A U
B L E E D I N G S D K R
L E B B R O T U C E O E
I G L Q U E F L I M K D
C A O H F S R X E I O I
I C O R N P G D N C M S
T Y D A I D S E T L O E
Y A R D E C I S I O N A
O T I L L N E S S T W S
I G A T R I A L T Y L E
```

Congressional Ryan White CARE Act

Presidential Commission on AIDS

Color My World

Famous Words of Wisdom

"Listening to medical facts was not enough. People wanted one hundred percent guarantees. Because of the lack of education on AIDS, discrimination, fear, panic, and lies surrounded me. We had great faith that with patience, understanding, and education, that my family and I could be helpful in changing their minds and attitudes around."

—*Ryan White, testifying before the President's Commission on AIDS, 1988*

Doodle Space

Super Citizens

Samantha Smith

born 1972

Dear Mr. Andropov,

My name is Samantha Smith. I am ten years old. Congratulations on
your new job. I have been worrying about Russia and the United States
getting into a nuclear war. Are you going to vote to have a war or not?
If you aren't please tell me how you are going to help to not have a war.
This question you do not have to answer, but I would like to know why
you want to conquer the world or at least our country.
God made the world for us to live together in peace and not to fight.

Sincerely,
Samantha Smith

America's Goodwill Ambassador...

Samantha Smith was born in 1972 in a small town in Maine right on the border with Canada.

At that time, the United States was a part of what historians call the Cold War, which was a time of tension between the superpowers—the US and the Soviet Union (USSR)—and their allies (friends). The main aspect of the Cold War was that both sides, particularly the superpowers, were heavily armed with nuclear weapons, and both sides knew it. People who lived in the United States—even kids—knew that Soviet missiles were pointed at important places in the United States, such as the capital, Washington, DC. (American missiles were pointed at the USSR too.) People understood that if those missiles came, they would destroy the world and everything in it.

Samantha Smith knew these facts too. When she was just 10 years old in 1982, the leader of the Soviet Union was Yuri Andropov. Many people in the United States were worried that Andropov would start a real war, not just a cold one. When Samantha saw a picture of him on the cover of a magazine, she asked her mother, "If people are so afraid of him, why doesn't someone write a letter asking whether he wants to have a war or not?"

Her mother said, "Why don't you?"

And so she did.

Her letter was published in the Soviet newspaper *Pravda*, and Samantha became famous in the USSR. Later she was invited to visit the country, and she spoke with many people about her concerns for peace. Her enthusiasm and optimism made her a very good ambassador of goodwill and friendship between the two countries.

You Know What?

What was the Cold War? This is the term historians used to describe tensions between powerful countries in the West (the United States and its Western European allies in NATO) and the powers in the Eastern Bloc (the Soviet Union and other communist states in Central and Eastern Europe). They called it cold because no actual shots were fired—although there were activities such as the building of the Berlin Wall, which separated East Berlin from West Berlin, in 1961. The Cold War started after World War II, and continued until the fall of the Soviet Union in 1991—not long after Samantha Smith visited.

Doodle Space

Samantha Smith
123 Street Road
Manchester Maine 14351

Yuri Andropov

Dear Mr. Andropov,

My name is Samantha Smith. I am ten years old. Congratulations on your new job. I have been worrying about Russia and the United States getting into a nuclear war. Are you going to vote to have a war or not? If you aren't please tell me how you are going to help to not have a war. This question you do not have to answer, but I would like to know why you want to conquer the world or at least our country. God made the world for us to live together in peace and not to fight

Sincerely,
Samantha Smith

Word Search

★★★

Here's a word search puzzle. Find words from the Super Citizen story going across, down, or diagonally. Circle any words you find:

ambassador	missiles	letter	USSR
goodwill	nuclear	enthusiasm	superpowers
Soviet Union	tension	optimism	peace
Cold War	Yuri Andropov	write	afraid
Europe	weapons	friendship	

```
Y A M R S C O L D W A R T
N U C L E A R X W R I T E
E B R O L E T T E R N G S
N O M I S S I L E S E O U
T A M B A S S A D O R O P
H U S S R N P E A C E D E
U F R I E N D S H I P W R
S D O P F E U R O P E I P
I G M T E N S I O N Y L O
A O P T I M I S M P A L W
S S O V I E T U N I O N E
M R S A W E A P O N S V R
O B A F R A I D R U K S S
```

You Can Be a Super Citizen Too!

★★

A good citizen tells the truth. And a good citizen obeys the law. A good citizen doesn't cheat either. That means you should do your own homework! Don't ever copy and paste from the Internet. Copying something someone else wrote or drew or photographed without their permission is called *plagiarism*—and it's against the law.

You Know What?

What is NATO? The letters stand for North Atlantic Treaty Organization, and the countries that are party to the treaty (signed on April 4, 1949) are in a military alliance with each other. There are 28 member states in NATO.

Famous Words of Wisdom

"Everyone in the Soviet Union who has known Samantha Smith will forever remember the image of the American girl who, like millions of Soviet young men and women, dreamt about peace, and about friendship between the peoples of the United States and the Soviet Union."

—*Mikhail Gorbachev, last leader of the Soviet Union*

You Know What?

A good citizen writes letters when she is concerned about the way the world is. This is the letter Samantha Smith wrote in 1982:

> Dear Mr. Andropov,
>
> My name is Samantha Smith. I am ten years old. Cogratulations on your new job. I have been worrying about Russia and the United States getting into a nuclear war. Are you going to vote to have a war or not? If you aren't please tell me how you are going to help to not have a war. This question you do not have to answer, but I would like to know why you want to conquer the world or at least our country. God made the world for us to live together in peace and not to fight.
>
> Sincerely,
>
> Samantha Smith

Famous Words of Wisdom

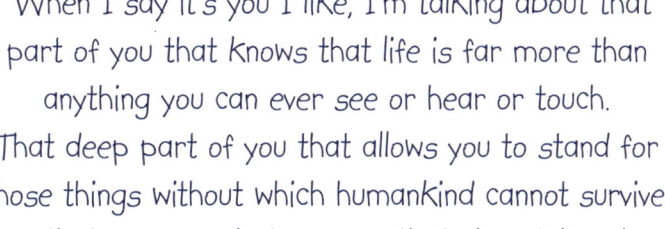

"When I say it's you I like, I'm talking about that part of you that knows that life is far more than anything you can ever see or hear or touch.
That deep part of you that allows you to stand for those things without which humankind cannot survive. Love that conquers hate, peace that rises triumphant over war, and justice that proves more powerful than greed."

—*Fred Rogers (Mr. Rogers), Commencement Address at Dartmouth College 9 June 2002*

You Know What?

In 1960, four black college freshmen—Ezell Blair Jr., 18; Franklin McCain, 19; Joseph McNeil, 18; and David Richmond, 18—began a "sit-in" at a segregated Woolworth's lunch counter in Greensboro, North Carolina. It was the beginning of the civil rights movement.

Who, What, When, Where

Why is the Statue of Liberty important? Draw it here!

Super Citizens

Zach Bonner

born 1996

He went door-to-door asking for help ...

Zach Bonner was born in Arkansas, but his family moved to Tampa, Florida, when he was in first grade. The next year (2004), Hurricane Charley hit southwest Florida—the strongest hurricane in that area in 40 years. Large trees, power lines and poles, smashed cars, and all sorts of debris littered the streets. Homes were destroyed. There was no electricity or running water.

But 7-year-old Zach thought he could help. He went door-to-door pulling his little red wagon, asking for food and water to help people who had lost everything in the storm. With the help of his friends and family, he eventually collected enough food and water donations to fill 27 trucks!

Zach got a good look at what it was like to be without a home when he saw what the hurricane did in Florida. And he saw the difference he could make in the lives of people who needed help— just one kid made a difference! The next year, with help from his family, Zach formed the nonprofit Little Red Wagon Foundation so he could accept more donations from people who were inspired by his work for those in need. Zach's foundation is designed to help children from poor families, especially kids who are homeless. One of his projects was collecting backpacks that were filled with supplies for homeless kids.

In 2007, when he was 10 years old, Zach began working to draw attention to the homeless. How? He walked from his home in Tampa to Tallahassee, the capital of Florida, to raise awareness, money, and resources for kids. That's about 250 miles. The next year he walked from Tallahassee to Atlanta, Georgia, and in 2009 Zach walked from Atlanta to Washington, DC. But he wasn't done! In 2010, at age 12, Zach walked from Florida to California—a March Across America. It took 6 months and covered 2,478 miles, but it got a lot of attention for homeless people.

Later, Zach lived for 7 days in a clear box near a mall, to show people what it was like to have to live out in the open, without a house. He encouraged people to donate canned food, which was given to local charities to distribute.

Zach received the Presidential Service Award in 2006, from President Bush. It's an award to honor people who have given a lot of time to help others. Zach believes kids can and should help other kids. Ask your parents if you can get involved with the Little Red Wagon Foundation!

Who, What, When, Where

★★

Recreate Zach's Walk Across America!

On the map below, draw a line from Tampa, Florida, to Tallahassee, and from Tallahassee to Atlanta, Georgia, and from there to Washington, DC. Ask your mom or dad for help to find a map online or in a book to find the other cities. Draw a second line from Tampa across the southern United States to Los Angeles, California.

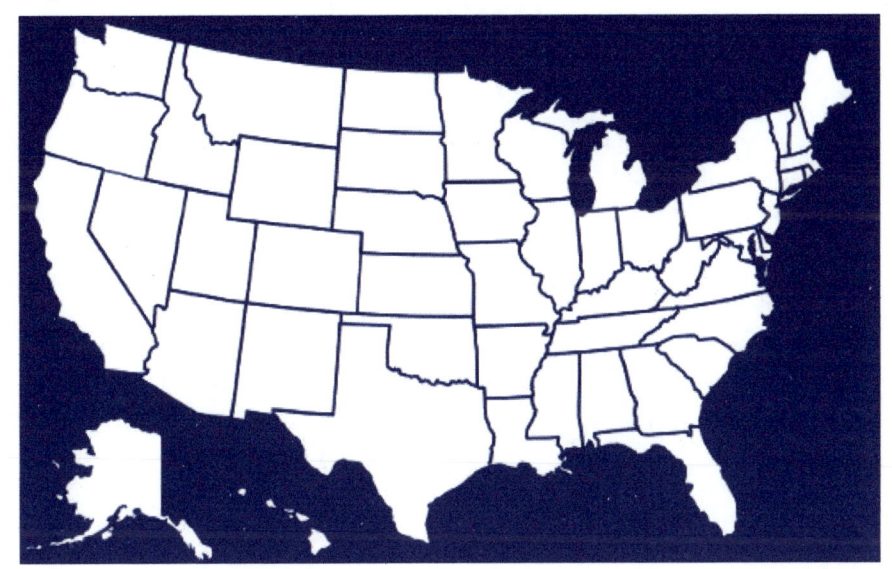

Answers:
1st trip: Florida, Georgia, South Carolina, North Carolina, Virginia, Maryland
2nd trip: Florida, Alabama, Mississippi, Louisiana, Texas, New Mexico, Arizona, California

Word Search

★★

Here's a word search puzzle. Find words from the Super Citizen story going across, down, or diagonally. Circle any words you find:

homeless	backpack	walk
wagon	donate	Washington
red	volunteer	charity
food	hurricane	service
water	Florida	kids

```
B U H E L P I N G R U F
A W V O L U N T E E R P
G B A C K P A C K D G I
L W K S E R V I C E N U
S E L W H O M E L E S S
V C H A R I T Y J N U D
M D E T P F N V O L B O
R I D E T I N G R F W N
F L O R I D A J T S F A
O K I D S W N E D O N T
O P J H U R R I C A N E
D M Y W A L K T O P B V
```

 # You Can Be a Super Citizen Too!

★★

Is there an extraordinary person in your community whose contributions have been overlooked? Why not nominate that person for a Super Citizen's Award? With your nomination, that person could be recognized for all they do.

Famous Words of Wisdom

"I just think about the kids. And that's what really keeps me going, because these kids, they're homeless and they don't get to just say, you know, "I'm tired of being homeless. Oh, well, I'm not going to be homeless anymore." So why should I get to quit walking or whatever project I'm doing?"

—*Zach Bonner, in an interview with Beliefnet, about why he continues to help others*

You Know What?

Who were the Founding Fathers? These men were political leaders in their communities in the 13 British colonies who became dissatisfied with the way King George treated his colonial subjects—and they ultimately led the American War of Independence. There are 7 Founding Fathers:

John Adams
Benjamin Franklin
Alexander Hamilton
James Monroe
Thomas Jefferson
James Madison
George Washington

You Know What?

Name the state for each capital city: List STATES next to the capitals.

Albany _____

Annapolis _____

Atlanta _____

Augusta _____

Austin _____

Baton Rouge _____

Bismarck _____

Boise _____

Boston _____

Carson City _____

Charleston _____

Cheyenne _____

Columbia _____

Columbus _____

Concord _____

Denver _____

Des Moines _____

Dover _____

Frankfort _____

Harrisburg _____

Hartford _____

Helena _____

Honolulu _____

Indianapolis _____

Jackson _____

Jefferson City _____

Juneau _____

Lansing _____

Lincoln _____

Little Rock _____

Madison _____

Montgomery _____

Montpelier _____

Nashville _____

Oklahoma City ____

Olympia _____

Phoenix _____

Providence _____

Raleigh _____

Richmond _____

Sacramento _____

Salem _____

Salt Lake City _____

Santa Fe _____

Sioux Falls _____

Springfield _____

St. Paul _____

Tallahassee _____

Topeka _____

Trenton _____

Answers:

Albany, NY
Annapolis, MD
Atlanta, GA
Augusta, ME
Austin, TX
Baton Rouge, LA
Bismarck, ND
Boise, ID
Boston, MA
Carson City, NV
Charleston, WV
Cheyenne, WY
Columbia, SC

Columbus, OH
Concord, NH
Denver, CO
Des Moines, IA
Dover, DE
Frankfort, KY
Harrisburg, PA
Hartford, CT
Helena, MT
Honolulu, HI
Indianapolis, IN
Jackson, MS
Jefferson City, MO

Juneau, AK
Lansing, MI
Lincoln, NE
Little Rock, AR
Madison, WI
Montgomery, AL
Montpelier, VT
Nashville, TN
Oklahoma City, OK
Olympia, WA
Phoenix, AZ
Providence, RI
Raleigh, NC

Richmond, VA
Sacramento, CA
Salem, OR
Salt Lake City, UT
Santa Fe, NM
Sioux Falls, SD
Springfield, IL
St. Paul, MN
Tallahassee, FL
Topeka, KS
Trenton, NJ

Songs about America

The Star-Spangled Banner

[https://www.youtube.com/watch?v=vPKp29Luryc]

Declared our National Anthem in 1931, the words to "The Star-Spangled Banner," are from a poem written by Francis Scott Key called "Defense of Fort McHenry" in 1814. It's set to the tune of a song popular in Great Britain at the time.

O say can you see, by the dawn's early light,
What so proudly we hailed at the twilight's last gleaming,
Whose broad stripes and bright stars through the perilous fight,
O'er the ramparts we watched, were so gallantly streaming?
And the rockets' red glare, the bombs bursting in air,
Gave proof through the night that our flag was still there;
O say does that star-spangled banner yet wave
O'er the land of the free and the home of the brave?

 # You Can Be a Super Citizen Too!

You can be a super citizen in you neighborhood, just by helping to keep it looking nice. If you see a piece of litter that has blown in your yard or neighbor's, you can help by picking up the trash and properly disposing of the litter.

You Know What?

The United States has had 43 elected presidents since 1789 (but 44 presidencies—because Grover Cleveland served 2 nonconsecutive terms).

1. George Washington (Virginia)
2. John Adams (Massachusetts)
3. Thomas Jefferson (Virginia)
4. James Madison (Virginia)
5. James Monroe (Virginia)
6. John Quincy Adams (Massachusetts)
7. Andrew Jackson (Tennessee)
8. Martin Van Buren (New York)
9. William Henry Harrison (Ohio)
10. John Tyler (Virginia)
11. James K. Polk (Tennessee)
12. Zachary Taylor (Louisiana)
13. Millard Fillmore (New York)
14. Franklin Pierce (New Hampshire)
15. James Buchanan (Pennsylvania)
16. Abraham Lincoln (Illinois)
17. Andrew Johnson (Tennessee)
18. Ulysses S. Grant (Illinois)
19. Rutherford B. Hayes (Ohio)
20. James A. Garfield (Ohio)
21. Chester A. Arthur (New York)
22. Grover Cleveland (New York)
23. Benjamin Harrison (Indiana)
24. Grover Cleveland (New York)
25. William McKinley (Ohio)
26. Theodore Roosevelt (New York)
27. William Howard Taft (Ohio)
28. Woodrow Wilson (New Jersey)
29. Warren G. Harding (Ohio)
30. Calvin Coolidge (Massachusetts)
31. Herbert Hoover (California)
32. Franklin D. Roosevelt (New York)
33. Harry S. Truman (Missouri)
34. Dwight D. Eisenhower (New York and Kansas)
35. John F. Kennedy (Massachusetts)
36. Lyndon B. Johnson (Texas)
37. Richard Nixon (New York and California)
38. Gerald Ford (Michigan)
39. Jimmy Carter (Georgia)
40. Ronald Reagan (California)
41. George H. W. Bush (Texas)
42. Bill Clinton (Arkansas)
43. George W. Bush (Texas)
44. Barack Obama (Illinois)

You Know What?

What's a monument? It's a structure—maybe a hall or other structure, a very old building, a statue, a pillar, even a landmark like a mountain—that is maintained as a memory of something or someone important. And there are monuments all over the country! Some are called National Historic Landmarks (mostly buildings and statues), others are called National Monuments (mostly land, natural wonders, or ancient structures). Here are just a few of the most famous outside of Washington, DC:

Statue of Liberty / New York Harbor, New York
Gateway Arch / St. Louis, Missouri
Mount Vernon / Alexandria, Virginia
Liberty Bell / Philadelphia, Pennsylvania
Mount Rushmore / Keystone, South Dakota
USS Arizona Memorial / Pearl Harbor, Honolulu, Hawaii
Little Bighorn Battlefield / Crow Agency, Montana
Alamo / San Antonio, Texas
Fort Sumter / Charleston Harbor, South Carolina
National September 11 Memorial / New York City, New York

Famous Words of Wisdom

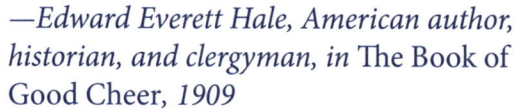

"I am only one; but still I am one. I cannot do everything; but still I can do something; and because I cannot do everything, I will not refuse to do the something that I can do."

—*Edward Everett Hale, American author, historian, and clergyman, in* The Book of Good Cheer, *1909*

 # You Can Be a Super Citizen Too!

★★

Do you have a special talent? You can be a super citizen by sharing your talent or skills with others! If you're good at math, why not ask your teacher if there's someone in your class who is struggling with math—maybe you could help them study for the next quiz. What's your special skill?

_____

Who, What, When, Where

★★

There are 8 states that begin with the letter M. Can you name them? Here are their abbreviations:

MO _____

MD _____

MN _____

MI _____

MA _____

MT _____

MS _____

ME _____

Answers: Missouri, Maryland, Minnesota, Michigan, Massachusetts, Montana, Mississippi, Maine

You Know What?

President John Quincy Adams spent much of his youth (11–17) accompanying his father, John Adams, on overseas diplomatic missions. He became fluent in several languages because he went to school in several countries.

Famous Words of Wisdom

"You learn something out of everything, and you come to realize more than ever that we're all here for a certain space of time, and then it's going to be over, and you better make this count."
—*Nancy Reagan*

You Can Be a Super Citizen Too!

Gratitude is heroic too! The *Mayflower* settlers were so thankful for the Native Americans who helped them, that they planned a harvest celebration. Today we call the celebration Thanksgiving. Why not keep a gratitude journal to write down everything for which you are grateful? Today I am grateful for _____

_____

_____

_____

_____

_____

Famous Words of Wisdom

"But you must remember, my fellow-citizens, that eternal vigilance by the people is the price of liberty, and that you must pay the price if you wish to secure the blessing."
—*Andrew Jackson, Farewell Address, 4 March 1837*

You Know What?

Martha Jefferson Randolph, Thomas Jefferson's daughter, was devoted to him. After her mother's death, she accompanied her father to Paris when he served as US Minister to France in 1785–1789. She was 12 when the trip started.

Famous Words of Wisdom

"I've spoken of the shining city all my political life, but I don't know if I ever quite communicated what I saw when I said it. But in my mind it was a tall proud city built on rocks stronger than oceans, wind-swept, God-blessed, and teeming with people of all kinds living in harmony and peace, a city with free ports that hummed with commerce and creativity, and if there had to be city walls, the walls had doors and the doors were open to anyone with the will and the heart to get here."
—*Ronald Reagan*

Famous Words of Wisdom

"The good particular men may do separately, in relieving the sick, is small, compared with what they may do collectively."
—Benjamin Franklin, "Appeal for the Hospital,"
The Pennsylvania Gazette, 8 August 1751

Who, What, When, Where

★★★

There are 4 states that begin with the letter A. Can you name them? Here are their abbreviations:

AR _____

AL _____

AK _____

AZ _____

Answers: Arkansas, Alabama, Alaska, Arizona

Famous Words of Wisdom

"Some boast of being friends to government; I am a friend to righteous government, to a government founded upon the principles of reason and justice; but I glory in publicly avowing my eternal enmity to tyranny."
—John Hancock, one of the Founding Fathers,
5 March 1774

Who, What, When, Where

★★★

Which state has supplied the most presidents?

_____

Which state comes in second in the presidential sweepstakes?

_____

There are 32 states that have never had a native son elected as president. Can you name them?

_____

_____

_____

_____

Answers: New York: 9
Ohio: 6
AL, AK, AZ, CO, CT, DE, FL, HI, ID, IA, KY, ME, MD, MN, MS, MT, NE, NV, NM, NC, ND, OK, OR, RI, SC, SD, UT, VT, WA, WV, WI, W

You Know What?

⋀⋀

The faces of George Washington, Thomas Jefferson, Theodore Roosevelt, and Abraham Lincoln make up the Mount Rushmore National Memorial—a huge sculpture carved into the granite face of a mountain in the Black Hills of South Dakota. It was constructed between 1935–1939.

★★

Map of the USA

This map has no state names! Can you name them? List states with numbers 1-50. Place the number in the appropriate state.

1 Alabama		26 Montana	
2 Alaska		27 Nebraska	
3 Arizona		28 Nevada	
4 Arkansas		29 New Hampshire	
5 California		30 New Jersey	
6 Colorado		31 New Mexico	
7 Connecticut		32 New York	
8 Delaware		33 North Carolina	
9 Florida		34 North Dakota	
10 Georgia		35 Ohio	
11 Hawaii		36 Oklahoma	
12 Idaho		37 Oregon	
13 Ilinois		38 Pennsylvania	
14 Indiana		39 Rhode Island	
15 Iowa		40 South Carolina	
16 Kansas		41 South Dakota	
17 Kentucky		42 Tennessee	
18 Louisiana		43 Texas	
19 Maine		44 Utah	
20 Maryland		45 Vermont	
21 Massachusetts		46 Virginia	
22 Michigan		47 Washington	
23 Minnesota		48 West Virginia	
24 Mississippi		49 Wisconsin	
25 Missouri		50 Wyoming	

SEE ANSWERS ON PAGE 176.

Songs about America

Hail, Columbia

[https://www.youtube.com/watch?v=JPlQS1pzHdA]

Before "The Star-Spangled Banner" was made the official national anthem, "Hail, Columbia" was one of several songs used at patriotic events. Philip Phile composed the music in 1789 for the inauguration ceremony of George Washington; lyrics by Joseph Hopkinson were added in 1798. This song is still used to announce the Vice President of the United States.

Hail Columbia, happy land!
Hail, ye heroes, heav'n-born band,
Who fought and bled in freedom's cause,
Who fought and bled in freedom's cause,
And when the storm of war was gone
Enjoy'd the peace your valor won.
Let independence be our boast,
Ever mindful what it cost;
Ever grateful for the prize,
Let its altar reach the skies.

Firm, united let us be,
Rallying round our liberty,
As a band of brothers joined,
Peace and safety we shall find.

[Verses 3, 4, and 5 can be found online.]

Famous Words of Wisdom

"Don't fire until you see the whites of their eyes!"
—*Israel Putnam, commanding his troops at the battle of Bunker Hill, 1775*

Who, What, When, Where

★★★

State trivia! Can you answer this?

1. Which is the largest state in the union?
2. Which is the largest state in the lower 48?
3. Which is the largest state east of the Mississippi River?
4. Which is the smallest state of all?
5. Which state has the longest coastline? The shortest?
6. What is the most populated state? The least?
7. Which state was the first to enter the union? The last?

Answers: 1. Alaska 2. Texas 3. Michigan 4. Rhode Island 5. Alaska, New Hampshire 6. California, Wyoming 7. Delaware, Hawaii

You Can Be a Super Citizen Too!

★★★

Your parents will think you're a hero if you help out at home and if you have a good attitude. When you have a good attitude, you'll be surprised at how the attitudes of others will change. Do you have a good attitude? Do you remember to say please and thank you?

Presidential Crossword Puzzle:
The H's Have It!

These presidents all have their name's first letter in common. Use the library or research online.

Across

1. There were 2 presidents by this name: grandfather and grandson.

Down

1. Our 19th president.
2. This Ohioan is often rated the worst president.
3. This president, a mining engineer, came to office without ever having held an elected office before.

Who, What, When, Where

★★★

Presidential trivia! Use the library or search online to answer these questions about US presidents!

1. Who was the first president born in the 20th century?

2. Who was the first president born a US citizen?

3. Who was the first president born outside the original 13 states?

4. Who was the first president born in a hospital?

5. Which president was the only one to be unanimously elected?

6. Which president never married?

7. Who was the first president to call his home in Washington, DC the White House?

8. Who was the first president born west of the Mississippi?

9. Who was the first president to ride a train?

10. Who was the first president to campaign by telephone?

11. Who was the first president to hold a press conference on television?

12. Which presidents were father and son?

13. Which presidents were (distant) cousins?

14. Which presidents were grandfather and grandson?

Answers: 1. John F. Kennedy (1917) 2. Martin Van Buren (1782, after the Declaration of Independence was signed) 3. Abraham Lincoln (Kentucky) 4. Jimmy Carter 5. George Washington 6. James Buchanan 7. Theodore Roosevelt 8. Herbert Hoover (Iowa) 9. Andrew Jackson 10. William McKinley 11. John F. Kennedy 12. John Adams and John Quincy Adams; George H. W. Bush and George W. Bush 13. Theodore Roosevelt and Franklin Roosevelt 14. William Harrison and Benjamin Harrison

Famous Words of Wisdom

"Our liberty can never be safe but in the hands of the people themselves."
— *Thomas Jefferson, in a letter to George Washington, 4 January 1786*

You Know What?

The United States was formed by 13 British colonies that declared independence from England in 1776. They were:

Connecticut	New York
Delaware	North Carolina
Georgia	Pennsylvania
Maryland	Rhode Island and
Massachusetts Bay	Providence Plantations
New Hampshire	South Carolina
New Jersey	Virginia

You Can Be a Super Citizen Too!

Do you receive an allowance or sometimes get money for your birthday? A super citizen takes care of his money, not only by spending wisely, but also by saving a portion.

You Know What?

Our nation's capital, Washington, DC, is chock-full of monuments and landmarks! You could spend days and days seeing them all. Here are a few of the most popular:

- Washington Monument
- Jefferson Memorial
- Vietnam Veterans Memorial
- Lincoln Memorial
- Marine Corps War Memorial
- White House
- Arlington National Cemetery
- Capitol Building
- National Mall
- Smithsonian Institution

Famous Words of Wisdom

"We the People of the United States, in Order to form a more perfect Union, establish Justice, insure domestic Tranquility, provide for the common defense, promote the general Welfare, and secure the Blessings of Liberty to ourselves and our Posterity, do ordain and establish this Constitution for the United States of America."
—*Preamble to the United States Constitution*

Who, What, When, Where

★★

Presidential trivia! Use the library or search online to answer these questions about US presidents!

1. Which president installed the first bathtub in the White House?

2. Which president got stuck in the White House bathtub?

3. Which president was born on the 4th of July?

4. Which presidents died on the 4th of July?

5. Who was the oldest president ever elected?

6. Who was the youngest president ever elected?

7. Who was the tallest president?

8. Who was the shortest president?

9. Which presidents married while in office?

10. Who was the first president to run against a female candidate?

11. Which presidents were assassinated?

12. Which presidents survived assassination attempts?

13. Which presidents—other than those assassinated—died in office?

14. Which presidents are buried in Arlington National Cemetery?

Answers: 1. Millard Fillmore **2.** William Howard Taft; a larger one was ordered **3.** Calvin Coolidge (1872) **4.** Thomas Jefferson (1826), John Adams (1826), James Monroe (1831) **5.** Ronald Reagan (age 69) **6.** John F. Kennedy (age 43) **7.** Abraham Lincoln (6 feet, 4 inches) **8.** James Madison (5 feet, 4 inches) **9.** John Tyler, Grover Cleveland, and Woodrow Wilson **10.** Ulysses S. Grant (Virginia Woodhull in 1872) **11.** Abraham Lincoln (1865), James Garfield (1881), William McKinley (1901), John F. Kennedy (1963) **12.** Andrew Jackson, Theodore Roosevelt, Franklin D. Roosevelt, Harry Truman, Gerald Ford, Ronald Reagan **13.** William Harrison (1841), Zachary Taylor (1850), Warren Harding (1923), Franklin D. Roosevelt (1945) **14.** William Howard Taft and John F. Kennedy

You Know What?

William Frederick "Buffalo Bill" Cody started working at the age of 11 after his father's death; he became a rider for the Pony Express at 14. During the American Civil War, he served for the Union, and during the Indian Wars he was a civilian scout. He received the Medal of Honor in 1872.

Famous Words of Wisdom

"Right is of no sex, Truth is of no color, God is the Father of us all, and we are all Brethren."
—*Frederick Douglass, in* The North Star
(antislavery newspaper), December 3, 1847

You Know What?

The Liberty Bell was ordered all the way from London and placed in the Pennsylvania State House in 1752. It was cast with the lettering "Proclaim LIBERTY throughout all the land unto all the inhabitants thereof," a Biblical reference. It got that famous crack sometime in the early 1800s, though how is another story lost to history. Today you can find it in Independence National Historical Park in Philadelphia.

Songs about America

Columbia, the Gem of the Ocean

[https://www.youtube.com/watch?v=siHfQGn3JTs]

This song was popular during the Civil War era, and was often played at important national events. It was written by Thomas á Becket Sr. in 1843.

O Columbia! the gem of the ocean,
The home of the brave and the free,
The shrine of each patriot's devotion,
A world offers homage to thee;
Thy mandates make heroes assemble,
When Liberty's form stands in view;
Thy banners make tyranny tremble,
When borne by the red, white, and blue.
When borne by the red, white, and blue,
When borne by the red, white, and blue,
Thy banners make tyranny tremble,
When borne by the red, white, and blue.

[Verses 2 and 3 can be found online.]

Famous Words of Wisdom

"So let us begin anew—remembering on both sides that civility is not a sign of weakness, and sincerity is always subject to proof. Let us never negotiate out of fear. But let us never fear to negotiate."
— *John F. Kennedy, Inaugural Address, 20 January 1961*

You Know What?

Have you ever been to a public library? It may have been a library funded by Andrew Carnegie, who migrated to the United States with his family in 1848, when he was just 12 years old. He found a job, but he spent his spare time in a library, reading and educating himself. By 1900—through hard work—he was one of the richest men in the world. He spent the rest of his life giving away his money, and he funded more than 2,500 libraries around the world.

Famous Words of Wisdom

"The gods of the valley are not the gods of the hills."
—*Ethan Allen, revolutionary, 21 January 1738-12 February 1789*

Who, What, When, Where

****

Can you match the US presidents with their nicknames? Use the library or research online.

James Buchanan	The Peanut Farmer
Chester A. Arthur	His Obstinacy
Jimmy Carter	Cautious Cal
Grover Cleveland	Bachelor President
Bill Clinton	Old Tippecanoe
Calvin Coolidge	Chet
Dwight D. Eisenhower	Old Hickory
William Henry Harrison	The Tennessee Taylor
Herbert Hoover	Ike
Andrew Jackson	Bubba
Andrew Johnson	The Great Engineer

James Buchanan: Bachelor President, Chester A. Arthur: Chet, Jimmy Carter: The Peanut Farmer, Grover Cleveland: His Obstinacy, Bill Clinton: Bubba, Calvin Coolidge: Cautious Cal, Dwight D. Eisenhower: Ike, William Henry Harrison: Old Tippecanoe, Herbert Hoover: The Great Engineer, Andrew Jackson: Old Hickory, Andrew Johnson: The Tennessee Taylor

Doodle Space

You Know What?

The National September 11 Memorial & Museum commemorate two events: the September 11, 2001, attacks that killed 2,977 people, and the World Trade Center bombing of 1993, which killed 6. It is located at the site of the former World Trade Center.

Famous Words of Wisdom

"By the rude bridge that arched the flood,
Their flag to April's breeze unfurled,
Here once the embattled farmers stood,
And fired the shot heard round the world."

—*from "Concord Hymn," a poem by Ralph Waldo Emerson, 1837*

 # You Can Be a Super Citizen Too!

You may have heard a little rhyme that begins "Sticks and stones may break my bones...." But the truth is, thoughtless words can and do hurt others. A super citizen is careful when speaking, because they do not want to hurt anyone's feelings. Remember, if you are wrong, say you are sorry.

Who, What, When, Where

★★

First Lady trivia! Use the library or search online to answer these questions about the wives of US presidents! Use the library or research online.

Which First Lady was the first to earn a college degree?

Which First Lady was the first to earn a graduate degree?

How many First Ladies have earned college degrees?

Who was the first presidential widow to remarry?

Which First Ladies died while their husbands were in office?

Who was the first First Lady to fly in an airplane?

Which First Lady was a British subject?

Who is the only First Lady born outside of the United States?

Answers: Lucy Webb Hayes

Pat Nixon

12: Lucy Webb Hayes, Frances Folsom Cleveland, Caroline Harrison, Grace Coolidge, Lou Henry Hoover, Jacqueline Bouvier Kennedy, Ladybird Johnson, Pat Nixon, Nancy Davis Reagan, Hillary Rodham Clinton, Laura Bush, Michelle Obama

Frances Folsom Cleveland

Letitia Tyler (1842), Caroline Harrison (1892), and Ellen Wilson (1914)

Eleanor Roosevelt

Elizabeth Kortright Monroe

Louisa Adams (London, England)

You Know What?

Americans were fascinated by the news that the Montgolfier brothers had created and flown a hot-air balloon in 1783. In Baltimore the next year, Peter Carnes built a balloon but was too heavy to go up. But 13-year-old Edward Warren volunteered, and on June 23, 1784, Edward became the first American to ascend in a manned balloon.

Famous Words of Wisdom

"Liberty cannot be preserved without a general knowledge among the people ... Let us dare to read, think, speak and write."

—*John Adams, in his* Dissertation on the Cannon and Feudal Law *(1765)*

You Know What?

The Alamo Mission was built in 1724 in what was then Mexico, but during the Texas Revolution, Texians (colonists from the United States) were using it as a fortress when the Mexican army laid siege to it for 13 days and finally overran it in 1836. All the men inside were killed, including frontier heroes Davy Crockett and James Bowie.

You Know What?

The Boy Scouts of America, founded in 1910, is an organization whose mission is to help boys become responsible citizens, develop their characters, and learn self-reliance. Scouts—kids—do good deeds to help out. For example:

During World War I, Boy Scouts ...
- Sold Liberty bonds and war savings stamps totaling more than $355 million.
- Collected 100 railroad cars full of nutshells and peach pits for gas mask manufacturing
- Planted 12,000 Boy Scout war gardens

During World War II, Boy Scouts ...
- Collected 30 million pounds of rubber during a two-week drive
- 20,000 Scouts earned the Gen. Douglas MacArthur Medal for Victory Gardens
- Collected aluminum, wastepaper, and salvage
- Distributed air-raid posters
- Served as fire watchers

Songs about America

My Country, 'Tis of Thee

https://www.youtube.com/watch?v=u0ywDLpfBHg

While this song uses the same melody as the United Kingdom's "God Save the Queen," the lyrics were written by Samuel Francis Smith, a Baptist minister, journalist, and author. The song was first performed in public on July 4, 1831, in Boston, Massachusetts.

My country, 'tis of thee,
Sweet land of liberty,
Of thee I sing;
Land where my fathers died,
Land of the pilgrims' pride,
From ev'ry mountainside
Let freedom ring!

My native country, thee,
Land of the noble free,
Thy name I love;
I love thy rocks and rills,
Thy woods and templed hills;
My heart with rapture thrills,
Like that above.

Let music swell the breeze,
And ring from all the trees
Sweet freedom's song;
Let mortal tongues awake;
Let all that breathe partake;
Let rocks their silence break,
The sound prolong.

Our fathers' God to Thee,
Author of liberty,
To Thee we sing.
Long may our land be bright,
With freedom's holy light,
Protect us by Thy might,
Great God our King.

Famous Words of Wisdom

"The most important thing we can do is inspire young minds and to advance the kind of science, math, and technology education that will help youngsters take us to the next phase of space travel."

—*John Glenn, astronaut, on CNN,*
4 May 2000

 # You Can Be a Super Citizen Too!

★★★

A super citizen should know what's going on in the world. The television and Internet are great ways to stay aware of what's going on in the news. Remember, your parents will help you find a safe news source that's good for you. Talk with your parents about things you have heard or read, so they can help you understand things you may not understand.

Doodle Space

You Can Be a Super Citizen Too!

★★

A super citizen is always ready to help others. Does a neighbor need help with dog sitting, raking leaves, or taking the garbage bin to the street? There are many ways you can help others. Just be sure to seek your parent's approval.

Who, What, When, Where

★★

First Lady trivia! Use the library or search online to answer these questions about the wives of US presidents!

Who was the first First Lady to live in the White House?

Who is the only First Lady to speak an Asian language?

Which First Lady is the youngest wife of a sitting president?

Which First Lady had the largest age gap from her presidential husband?

Who was the first presidential spouse to hold press conferences?

Which First Lady was the longest-lived?

Which First Lady was the first to own and drive a car?

Which First Lady was the first to wear pants in public?

Answers: Abigail Adams, Louise (Lou) Hoover (Chinese), Frances Folsom Cleveland (age 21), Julia Gardiner Tyler (30 years), Eleanor Roosevelt, Bess Truman (age 97), Helene Taft, Pat Nixon

Presidential Crossword Puzzle: To a T!

These presidents all have their name's first letter in common. Use the library or research online.

Across

1. This president was a military hero of the Mexican-American War.

Down

1. After he was president, he was chief justice of the Supreme Court.
2. A presidential death made this man the first vice president to succeed to the presidency without being elected.
3. This president made the decision to drop an atomic bomb during World War II.

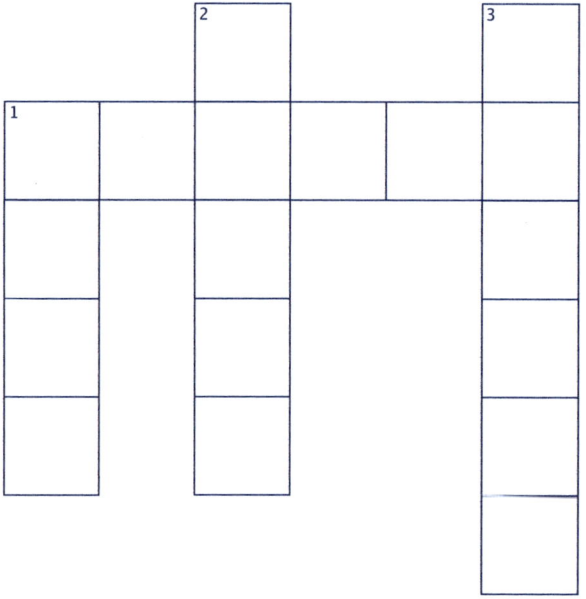

Answers:

Across
1. Taylor

Down
1. Taft
2. Tyler
3. Truman

You Know What?

Presidents who were also Boy Scouts:

George W. Bush: Cub Scout
Bill Clinton: Cub Scout
Gerald Ford: Eagle Scout
Lyndon B. Johnson: Scout leader
John F. Kennedy: Boy Scout & Scout leader
Franklin D. Roosevelt: Scout leader
Theodore Roosevelt: Boy Scouts of America founder
William Howard Taft: Boy Scouts of America founder

You Know What?

Here are some notable women who were Girl Scouts:

Madeleine Albright (former Secretary of State)
Barbara Bush (former First Lady)
Laura Bush (former First Lady)
Rosalynn Carter (former First Lady)
Hillary Clinton (former Secretary of State, former First Lady)
Lou Henry Hoover (former First Lady)
Pat Nixon (former First Lady)
Michelle Obama (First Lady)
Nancy Reagan (former First Lady)
Condoleezza Rice (former Secretary of State)
Edith Wilson (former First Lady)
... and virtually every female astronaut ever!

Songs about America

The Battle Hymn of the Republic
[https://www.youtube.com/watch?v=ORsNiReoCsw]

It was written during the American Civil War by Julia Ward Howe—a prominent abolitionist, social activist, and poet—to be sung to the tune that was already popular in 19th-century America. It was so popular, in fact, it was used in two other songs—"Glory, Hallelujah" and "John Brown's Body."

Mine eyes have seen the glory of the coming of the Lord;
He is trampling out the vintage where the grapes of wrath are stored;
He hath loosed the fateful lightning of His terrible swift sword:
His truth is marching on.

(Chorus)
Glory, glory, hallelujah!
Glory, glory, hallelujah!
Glory, glory, hallelujah!
His truth is marching on.

I have seen Him in the watch fires of a hundred circling camps,
They have builded Him an altar in the evening dews and damps;
I can read His righteous sentence by the dim and flaring lamps:
His day is marching on.

In the beauty of the lilies Christ was born across the sea,
With a glory in His bosom that transfigures you and me.
As He died to make men holy, let us live to make men free,
While God is marching on.

Famous Words of Wisdom

"Four score and seven years ago our fathers brought forth on this continent a new nation, conceived in liberty, and dedicated to the proposition that all men are created equal."

— *Abraham Lincoln, Gettysburg Address, November 19, 1863*

You Know What?

The Girl Scouts of the USA was founded in 1912, and the organization aims to empower girls and teach important values like honesty, courage, compassion, fairness, and citizenship. During the Great Depression of the 1930s, Girl Scouts collected clothing and food for those in need. Like the Boy Scouts, during World War II Girl Scouts acted as bicycle couriers, collected fat and scrap metal, and grew backyard gardens (known as Victory Gardens) to contribute to the war effort.

Famous Words of Wisdom

"We here highly resolve that these dead shall not have died in vain—that this nation, under God, shall have a new birth of freedom—and that government of the people, by the people, for the people, shall not perish from the earth."

—*Abraham Lincoln, Gettysburg Address, November 19, 1863*

You Know What?

Today we take our mail delivery for granted, but in the first half of the 1800s, it took weeks—sometimes months—for mail to travel between the eastern United States and the western states. Enter the Pony Express. In 1860, the first riders left St. Joseph, Missouri—as far west as the nation's rail system traveled—headed for Sacramento, California. It was a dangerous job, riding a horse alone over empty wilderness, facing weather extremes and the occasional Indian attack. The company advertised for "Young, skinny, wiry fellows not over 18. Must be expert riders willing to risk death daily. Orphans preferred." The Pony Express lasted about a year and a half—it was replaced by the transcontinental telegraph in late 1861 and the transcontinental railroad a few years later.

Famous Words of Wisdom

"This is preeminently the time to speak the truth, the whole truth, frankly and boldly. Nor need we shrink from honestly facing conditions in our country today. This great Nation will endure as it has endured, will revive and will prosper. So, first of all, let me assert my firm belief that the only thing we have to fear is fear itself."

—*Franklin Delano Roosevelt, First Inaugural Address, March 4, 1933*

 # You Can Be a Super Citizen Too!

Have you heard of the Golden Rule? That means you should treat others the way you want to be treated. A super citizen is kind in word and deed, and respectful of the differences others may have from you.

You Know What?

James Madison Randolph (b. 1806) was the first child born in the White House. His mother, Martha Jefferson Randolph was visiting her father, Thomas Jefferson, in Washington, DC at the President's House (now known as the White House) at the time.

Famous Words of Wisdom

"Give me your tired, your poor,
Your huddled masses yearning to breathe free,
The wretched refuse of your teeming shore.
Send these, the homeless, tempest-tost to me,
I lift my lamp beside the golden door!"

—*from "The New Colossus," a poem written in 1883 by Emma Lazarus to help pay for the pedestal of the Statue of Liberty.*

You Know What?

When Abraham Lincoln was a boy, he borrowed a book from a neighbor. (Books were scarce in those days, and expensive.) The book was accidentally ruined by rain, and young Lincoln went to the neighbor, told him what had happened—and spent the next three days working for the man to pay for the damage to the book. This was only the beginning of Lincoln's reputation for honesty.

Here are the mottos of the branches and units of the United States military:

Air Force: Above All

Army: This We'll Defend

Army Corps of Engineers: Essayons (Let us try)

Army Rangers: Sua Sponte (Of Their Own Accord)

Green Berets (Army Special Forces): De Oppresso Liber (To liberate the oppressed)

Coast Guard: Semper Paratus (Always Prepared)

Marine Corps: Semper Fidelis (Always Loyal)

National Guard: Always ready, always there

Navy: Non sibi sed patriae (Not for self, but for country)

Navy SEALS: The only easy day was yesterday

Seabees (Navy): Construimus, Batuimus (We Build, We Fight)

US Coast Guard Academy: Scientiae Cedit Mare (The sea yields to knowledge)

US Merchant Marine Academy: Acta Non Verba (Deeds not Words)

US Military Academy (West Point): Duty, Honor, Country

US Naval Academy: Ex Scientia Tridens (From Knowledge, Sea Power)

You Know What?

The Great Seal of the United States features a bald eagle holding 13 arrows in one talon and an olive branch in the other—symbols of war and peace. In its beak the eagle holds a scroll reading *E pluribus unum* ("out of many, one"). The Great Seal is used to authenticate documents issued by the United States government. It was first used in 1782, and is kept by the Secretary of State.

Famous Words of Wisdom

"Oh, give me a home where the Buffalo roam
Where the Deer and the Antelope play;
Where seldom is heard a discouraging word,
And the sky is not cloudy all day."

—from an 1873 poem by Brewster M. Higley called "My Western Home," which later became the song "Home on the Range"

Doodle Space

Famous Words of Wisdom

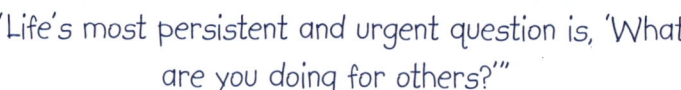

"Life's most persistent and urgent question is, 'What are you doing for others?'"

—*Martin Luther King Jr., on the community of man*

You Know What?

Is there a town named Columbia (or Columbus) near where you live? You'll find them all over the United States. It originated from the name of Christopher Columbus and is a poetic, symbolic name for the United States that's been in use since the 1730s—when the original thirteen colonies got their start. There are at least two American patriotic songs—"Hail, Columbia" and "Columbia, the Gem of the Ocean"—that use Columbia to mean the United States. But look around! Columbia is used a lot here in the United States: Columbia University in New York, the District of Columbia (our national capital), and the Columbia River, just to name a few.

 # You Can Be a Super Citizen Too!

There are hospitals with lots of children who are recovering from serious medical conditions. With help from your parents, you could spend an afternoon, after school, making new friends at a children's hospital. Take your favorite book or game with you to share with them! A volunteer is a super citizen for sure!

Songs about America

America the Beautiful

[https://www.youtube.com/watch?v=EmP9LvHgcaA]

Many Americans love this song so much they wish it were our national anthem! The words were originally a poem called "Pikes Peak," written by Katharine Lee Bates, an English teacher and author, in 1895. Later the poem was set to the music of Samuel A. Ward, a church organist and choirmaster. The song was published in 1910 as "America the Beautiful."

O beautiful for spacious skies,
For amber waves of grain,
For purple mountain majesties
Above the fruited plain!
America! America!
God shed his grace on thee
And crown thy good with brotherhood
From sea to shining sea!

O beautiful for patriot dream
That sees beyond the years
Thine alabaster cities gleam
Undimmed by human tears!
America! America!
God shed his grace on thee
And crown thy good with brotherhood
From sea to shining sea!

Who, What, When, Where

★★

There are 4 states whose capitals are the names of former US presidents. Can you name them?

_____

_____

_____

_____

Answers: Jackson (MS), Jefferson City (MO), Lincoln (NE), Madison (WI)

Famous Words of Wisdom

"It is from numberless diverse acts of courage and belief that human history is shaped. Each time a man stands up for an ideal, or acts to improve the lot of others, or strikes out against injustice, he sends forth a tiny ripple of hope, and crossing each other from a million different centers of energy and daring, those ripples build a current that can sweep down the mightiest walls of oppression and resistance."

—*Robert F. Kennedy, Day of Affirmation Address in Capetown, South Africa, 6 June 1966*

Who, What, When, Where

★★

Why is the Eagle used so often as a symbol in American History?
Draw one here!

American History Timeline

★★

A short list of events over 400+ years.
Add events you remember and think are important.

1492   Christopher Columbus lands in America.

1565   Saint Augustine, Florida, settled by the Spanish, becomes the first permanent European colony in North America.

1607   Jamestown, the first permanent English settlement in America.

1620   The Plymouth Colony in Massachusetts is established by the Pilgrims.

1754-63 French and Indian War.

1774   First Continental Congress.

1775-83 American Revolution: War of Independence.

1776   Continental Congress adopts the Declaration of Independence.

1777   Continental Congress approves the first official flag of the United States.

1789   George Washington is unanimously elected president of the United States.

1790   The Supreme Court meets for the first time.

1791   Bill of Rights is ratified.

1800   US Capital moves from Philadelphia to Washington, D.C.

American History Timeline Cont.

★★

1804   Lewis and Clark expedition.

1812-14   War of 1812. Francis Scott Key writes the "Star Spangled Banner."

1828   First public railroad is constructed.

1830   President Andrew Jackson signs Indian Removal Act. "Trail of Tears" begins 1838.

1831   *Liberator Newspaper* launches abolition of slavery movement.

1836   Texas declares independence from Mexico.

1846   USA declares war on Mexico.

1848   Gold rush begins in California.

1852   *Uncle Tom's Cabin* published.

1860   Abraham Lincoln elected President.

1861-65   Civil War.

1865   Abraham Lincoln assassinated.

1870   15th Amendent to the Constitution giving African Americans the right to vote.

1876   General Custer is killed in Montana.

1882   Congress establishes Standard times for regions in states.

American History Timeline Cont.

★★

1876   Statue of Liberty is dedicated.

1898   Spanish-American War.

1903   Panama Canal begins. Finished in 1918.

1908   Federal Bureau of Investigation (FBI) is created.

1914-18   World War I.

1915   First long-distance phone call from New York to San Francisco.

1918   World-wide flu kills 20 million people.

1919   League of Nations meets for the first time.

1927   Charles Lindbergh makes the first solo nonstop transatlantic flight in his plane *The Spirit of St. Louis.*

1931   "Star-Spangled Banner" chosen as national anthem.

1932   First woman (Hattie Carraway) elected to Congress.

1939-45   World War II.

1945   United Nations established.

1950-53   Korean War.

1958   *Explorer I,* first American satellite, is launched.

1959   Alaska and Hawaii become states.

American History Timeline Cont.

★★

1962   Lt. Col. John Glenn becomes first astronaut to orbit Earth.

1963   Martin Luther King Jr. delivers his "I Have a Dream" speech.

1964   President Lyndon Johnson signs Civil Rights Act.

1968   Martin Luther King Jr. is assassinated.

1973   President Richard Nixon resigns (Watergate) and Gerald Ford becomes President.

1986   Space shuttle *Challenger* explodes 73 seconds after liftoff.

1991   Persian Gulf War.

1995   Federal building in Oklahoma City is bombed killing 168.

1999   School shooting in Columbine, CO.

2002   President Bush declares war on the Middle East.

2002   Space shuttle *Columbia* explodes upon reentry into Earth's atmosphere.

2006   US Census Bureau estimates the population reaches 300 million.

2008   Barack Obama is elected first African-American President.

Activity on pages 140-141!